SIMPLE ITALIAN

To Mamma,
and my late Nonna Pina
and Nonna Irene,
whose culinary heritage
I treasure and strive
to pass on.

SIMPLE ITALIAN

THE ESSENTIALS of ITALIAN HOME COOKING

Silvia Colloca

plum. Pan Macmillan Australia

CONTENTS

Introduction

The simple truth is that everyone can, and should, cook!

It is my fervent conviction that cooking is a fundamental life skill that every one of us should practise. You can only really appreciate the intrinsic value and meaning of the food on your table when it is your hands that produced it. Cooking shouldn't feel like a chore or an obligation, but rather a creative, nurturing ritual. And I know all too well that in our busy lives, our jobs, family and social calendars often mean we have less time to prepare meals, but even setting aside a couple of days a week where we actively choose not to order in or eat out can be beneficial. It doesn't matter whether we opt for an elaborate, multi-course dining experience or a simple bruschetta with fresh tomatoes – they both achieve the same goal and are equally valid.

In my day-to-day life I have met a staggering number of adults who are convinced they can't cook. Maybe they tried once or twice and it didn't work so they lost confidence and quit. Or maybe they grew up in a household where meal preparation was seen as a necessity, and never a joy. I know that cooking feels daunting for some, and it is easy to find excuses and claim we are time poor (yet then spend time driving to a restaurant, fighting for a parking spot and waiting for our food to be cooked by someone else).

In my experience, everyone can cook; no one is too young or too old to learn a few uncomplicated recipes, to spark an initial flame that could turn into a burning passion for home cooking. Start with simple dishes that will reward you with quick gratification, like a nourishing dish of greens (see page 198) served with grilled bread, a one-pot pasta (see pages 58–65) or a humble frittata (see page 158). Once you start you'll be on your way to catching the cooking bug, and before you know it you will be rolling out gnocchi (see page 91), hand cutting pappardelle (see page 36) or roasting a whole fish (see page 177). Italian home cooking is the perfect gateway to this sensory universe, as its frugal nature – what Italians call 'cucina povera' (peasant-style cooking) – is nourishing, accessible and cost effective, not to mention incredibly delicious.

Italian home cooking is simple, but that should not be confused with simplistic or lazy. Creating delightful dishes using just three or four everyday ingredients requires resourcefulness, a genuine love for produce and equal parts skill and instinct. I have acquired a wealth of knowledge just by observing my mamma and two nonnas create sensational meals with very little, and I constantly add to this knowledge by seeing what others are making, and the way they use and combine their ingredients. For me, simple always triumphs over complicated.

Simple is beautiful. *Simple* means you can pick up this book and cook all the dishes without fear of failing. You don't need to have a single drop of Italian blood in your veins to approach home cooking like Italians do, nor do you need to have inherited family recipes from older generations.

Take mine and make them yours. It's that simple.

Silvia x

A NOTE ON INGREDIENT QUANTITIES AND OVEN TEMPERATURES

When I submitted the manuscript for this book to my incredibly patient and meticulous editor Rachel, she returned it with many question marks around ingredient quantities; it seems my vague instructions to add a couple of handfuls of this or a few pinches of that didn't quite cut it. In fairness, over the years I have learned to be more precise when offering measurements, as I know some home cooks feel more comfortable with specific quantities. But this book has to allow for a few exceptions, because Italian home cooking was created without scales or measuring cups. Our nonnas and mammas cook with their hands and eyes, and nothing terrible will happen to your pesto Genovese if you add an extra teaspoon of pine nuts or a few extra basil leaves. Try to approach cooking like an Italian: use the recipes and the ingredient quantities as a guide, and then go with your own flow. My mamma's carbonara is slightly different from my brother's, yet they both use exactly the same ingredients. It doesn't matter in the least because they both turn out beautifully. Italian home cooking has many virtues, and being very forgiving is certainly one of them!

On a technical note, all oven temperatures in this book are conventional. If you are using a fan-forced oven, you will need to reduce the temperature by about 20°C. All ovens vary, so you may need to adjust baking times accordingly.

PASTA
perfection

A book about Italian home cooking would not make sense without an extensive chapter on our favourite carb.

In Itallan cooking we have a pasta shape for every occasion and any mood – each and every one of them serving a specific purpose. We match them with the sauces they are best suited to be coated with, in an ideal marriage of the senses that epitomises one fundamental principle of Italian home cooking: simple food makes everyone happy.

Pasta is so deeply embedded in Italian culture, it's never just a recipe – it's a legacy that is shared every day. What may seem like a very basic pasta al sugo (with tomato sauce) is the expression of a culture that has thrived on recreating the same sauce, the same pasta for centuries. I can't think of a single day when Nonna Irene wouldn't make this simple meal for us. It was economical, nutritious and delicious, but most importantly it created a sense of familiarity and safety, as if the smell of the sweet tomatoes simmering away would cast a protective spell over her family. To this day, two decades after her passing, she still lives on in my kitchen when I make her sauce. To me, it's a true expression of love.

But of course Italian nonnas are also very practical and, along with conjuring charms, they hold that sought-after knowledge of how to get your pasta just right. It is not simply a matter of making a dough or cooking rigatoni perfectly al dente; they recognise the virtues of every pasta shape, and know what to pair it with to achieve the perfect union of flavour and texture.

Growing up in Italy, I learned a lot by observing my nonnas, my aunties and my mamma, and I am here to pass my insights on to you.

The world of pasta is so wide and diverse, it's difficult to settle on the 'essentials'. The recipes in this chapter are *my* essentials, and I apologise if your favourite ones are not represented. But no matter where your loyalties lie, it is crucial to establish a few rules about making pasta – please turn the page for my ten non-negotiable ones for achieving perfect pasta every time.

Whether you were born into an Italian household or simply have a passion for the wonderful world of pasta, I hope you find this chapter helpful. For us Italians it's not 'just a meal', it's a ritual that unites family and friends. And in this fast-paced world, this seems like the greatest gift of all.

Note: This chapter includes my essential pasta recipes only. If you would like to learn about how Italians incorporate baby pasta or fresh pasta into soups, please see page 213.

My 10 Rules for Perfect Pasta

1. SALT THE WATER. Have you ever seen an Italian salting the pasta cooking water? We go by the fistful. This is because salt is actually part of your overall seasoning. No matter how spectacular the sauce is, if you don't salt the water enough the pasta will be bland and, therefore, the whole dish will be bland. Your pasta cooking water should taste almost as salty as the sea.

It doesn't matter when you salt it. You can wait for the water to come to the boil, add the salt and stir, then wait until it comes back to a rolling boil before adding the pasta, or you can add salt to cold water and bring it to the boil. If you do this, make sure you stir the salt well until it dissolves; otherwise it can settle on the bottom of your pan and act as a corrosive. I should also add that pasta needs to be cooked in plenty of water, so use a big pan!

2. DON'T ADD OIL TO THE WATER. If you do, the oil will float to the top, rendering it completely useless, then when you drain your pasta the oil coating will prevent the sauce from adhering properly. The only way to stop pasta from sticking together is to boil it in plenty of salted water, making sure you stir as you drop it in and a few times as it cooks.

3. NEVER BREAK YOUR SPAGHETTI OR LONG PASTA! Unless you are using your long strands as an addition to a soup, you should never break them so they fit in the pan more easily. Just use a bigger pan! Long pasta, such as spaghetti, linguine, tagliatelle and tagliolini, are designed to be twirled around a fork, enveloped in the sauce, thus creating a fabulous and satisfying mouthful. As with every rule there is one exception, and that is if you are making ziti with Genovese sauce (see page 54), where the pasta is broken by hand. Just to make things confusing!

4. BOIL, DON'T SIMMER! Never cook your pasta over low heat or it will turn into a gluey mess. A fierce rolling boil is what is needed.

5. DON'T OVERCOOK YOUR PASTA. This is probably the most important rule of all. Italians take the concept of al dente extremely seriously. It literally translates as 'to the tooth' and that's an accurate indication of how you need to cook it. As a rule of thumb, al dente means cooking pasta for a minute or two less than you would instinctively think.

Once your pasta is overcooked there is no saving it, and no sauce – however delicious – can repair the damage. This particularly applies to packaged dried pasta, which Italians consume most days. Check the suggested cooking time on the packet, then slash it by 60–90 seconds. Once the pasta is removed from the water, the residual heat will continue the cooking process, and if you are tossing the pasta in a sauce, that too will count as cooking time. All of which means that if you observe the packet instructions, your pasta will be overdone by the time you eat it.

The first few times you might think it's not right, that it needs a few more minutes, but trust me, the al dente texture will grow on you and allow you to better appreciate the flavour of the pasta itself. You'll probably dress it with less sauce for this very reason. And as a bonus, al dente pasta is easier to digest.

Fresh pasta is more forgiving with a softer texture than dried pasta, which is why it is particularly loved by youngsters.

6. DON'T DRAIN IT – YOUR COOKING WATER IS THE SECRET TO PERFECT PASTA! I personally like to use a spaghetti spoon or slotted spoon to drag the cooked pasta straight into the sauce, using the cooking water that comes with it to thicken the sauce. If you don't feel comfortable doing this, drain it in a colander, but reserve about a cup of the cooking water. It's full of starches and can really help bind the final dish together.

7 DON'T JUST SPOON THE SAUCE ON TOP AND 'THAT'S THAT'! Can you picture a bowl of pale noodles topped with a few tablespoons of red sauce, a dusting of parmigiano and a lone basil leaf? Okay, now try to unsee it! If you want to cook Italian food like an Italian, make sure your pasta spends time mingling with the sauce so that every single strand, every rigatoni tube is well coated. We never plate the pasta first and spoon the sauce on top – if we did, the undressed pasta would invariably stick together like glue. I promise you, a well-tossed pasta dish will look infinitely more appealing and taste a million times better.

8 DON'T DROWN IT! The sauce should coat the pasta evenly and lusciously, but not overwhelm it. If you have cooked your pasta to a perfect al dente, you will also want to taste its natural flavour. The sauce is a condiment so by all means be generous, but not wasteful. Speaking of which, if you are left with a little sauce on the plate, arm yourself with bread and mop away! We call this action 'scarpetta' (in Rome and in the south), 'intingolo' around Tuscany and 'puccia' in the north, where I grew up. Whatever you call it, it's a wonderful thing.

9 EAT IT STRAIGHT AWAY. When pasta is presented to the table in an Italian household, all the diners are already sitting down, fork in hand, eagerly ready to twirl some spaghetti or stab some orecchiette while they are still hot. Unless you are serving pasta as a cold salad (see page 78), which we often do in summer, your bowl of goodness needs to be consumed while still steaming. The main reason for this is that as the pasta cools down, it changes in texture, and so does the sauce. There is nothing less palatable than eating a plate of congealed eggy carbonara; and on the other hand, there's nothing quite as sensual as devouring it while still hot, with its natural creaminess lusciously coating every single pasta strand and the crispy guanciale salting your tongue. One other important reason is that, as explained in point 5, the residual heat within the pasta will continue cooking it ever so slightly. The more it sits, especially if it sits in a hot pan, the more it will cook.

10 PASTA IS NOT A SIDE DISH! Pasta is a main meal in its own right. On Italian menus you will find pasta (and sometimes rice) dishes under the name of 'primi patti'; these are first courses, and should not be confused with antipasto or entrees, and most certainly should never be treated as a side dish. Of course, if you love your chicken parma with a side of spaghetti, I'm not going to stop you from enjoying what is undoubtedly a satisfying meal, but let's all agree that it is not Italian. Wow, I got through this tricky paragraph without the use of capitals!

Fresh PASTA

Fresh pasta always features at an Italian festive table, whether it's a special celebration or a family Sunday lunch – any occasion that allows enough time to prepare it with love and care. Far from being hard to make, pasta dough can be hand kneaded and rolled quite easily. The dough can be assembled in a food processor to speed things up, but my preference is to always use my hands, as I find them to be my most reliable tool.

Fresh pasta dough is a combination of eggs and flour, or water and flour, with only a pinch of salt. No oil required. Once you feel comfortable with making the basic egg or vegan doughs in this chapter, feel free to experiment with different flours. I often cut type '00' flour with some wholemeal or spelt flour (see page 36) to give my pasta a bit of character. It may require a little more kneading and sometimes a few extra drops of water to make the dough more malleable, but you can build your expertise by experimenting with different textures. You can also try tinting your dough green or purple by adding a little processed spinach or beetroot, but keep in mind that if you add a liquid component you will have to adjust the quantity of flour as well. Whatever you decide, you want a smooth, pliable dough that can be rolled or shaped, but is not so soft that it becomes tacky.

Fresh pasta cooks far more quickly than its dried cousin, sometimes just a couple of minutes, and up to 5 minutes for dough made without eggs. Filled pasta also takes a little longer, depending on how thick the outer casing is. Please note that if fresh pasta is left to dry completely before cooking, you will have to add an extra minute or two to the cooking time. As for gauging when it's ready, it's important to know that fresh pasta behaves differently from dried. That famous 'al dente' texture generally refers to dried pasta. Perfectly cooked fresh pasta is softer but by no means sticky or gluey – it is its own marvellous, special-occasion self!

WHOLE-EGG pasta dough

Both my nonnas were fresh pasta magicians. They would roll out sheets of transparent pasta in a seemingly effortless way, beating the dough into silky submission through the sheer force of their hands. Although one was from Abruzzo and the other was from Emilia-Romagna, they both agreed on a ratio of 1 egg for every 100 g of flour, bridging the age-old gap between north and south. Stick with that and you will never get it wrong.

If you want to speed things up you can mix the dough in a food processor in a matter of minutes. Process the ingredients until they resemble wet sand, then tip onto a floured board or bench, bring together with your hands and knead for 3–4 minutes until smooth. Although this is not the way hardcore Italian nonnas operate, it yields a perfect result in a quarter of the time.

400 g (2⅔ cups) plain or
    type '00' flour
4 eggs, at room temperature
1 scant teaspoon salt flakes

SERVES 4

Place the flour on a board, make a well in the centre and drop in the eggs and salt. Combine using your fingers or a fork, then knead the mixture vigorously for about 10 minutes. At first it will look crumbly, but once your body heat activates the starch in the flour, the dough will change its texture, turning into a smooth, firm ball. Wrap it (I use beeswax wraps) and let it rest in the fridge for 20 minutes.

The rested dough can then be hand-rolled to the thickness you like. Or you can cut it into sections, roll it through a hand-cranked pasta machine and cut into your desired shape.

FRESH tagliatelle WITH roasted TOMATOES AND burrata

There is something deeply satisfying about watching a silky-smooth sheet of pasta go through the tagliatelle setting and come out the other end in perfect golden strands. Just be quick to catch them as they come through so they don't bunch up at the base of the machine. If, like me, you have eager youngsters on hand, enlist their help to make this process a fun family activity. On those days when you crave this dish but are pushed for time, feel free to use store-bought egg tagliatelle without any guilt whatsoever!

1 quantity Whole-egg Pasta Dough (see page 20)
plain flour and coarse semolina, for dusting
800 g cherry tomatoes
300 ml Quick and Easy Passata (see page 29)
3 tablespoons extra-virgin olive oil, plus extra for drizzling
handful of basil leaves, plus extra to serve
1 head of garlic, halved horizontally
salt flakes and freshly ground black pepper
1 burrata

SERVES 4

Make the pasta dough as instructed. After it has rested it will feel elastic and very pliable. Dust your board with flour or coarse semolina, and cut the dough into quarters. Work with one piece at a time and keep the rest wrapped up to prevent the dough from drying out. Flatten the dough with the palm of your hand, then pass it through the pasta machine's widest setting three or four times, folding the dough into three each time. Continue passing the dough through the machine (no further folding required), each time through a thinner setting, until you get to the second-last setting or the sheet is roughly 2.5 mm thick.

At this point, pass the dough sheet through the tagliatelle cutter. Gently place the cut noodles on a floured tea towel, dust with semolina and allow to dry slightly at room temperature. Repeat with the remaining portions of dough.

Meanwhile, preheat your oven to 180°C.

Toss the tomatoes, passata, olive oil, basil, garlic and some salt and pepper in a bowl, then spread out in a large baking dish. Roast for 35–40 minutes or until nice and saucy. The garlic will have gone soft, so you can squeeze one or two cloves into the sauce, if you like (save the rest for another use). Taste for seasoning and adjust to your liking.

Bring a large saucepan of salted water to the boil, drop in the tagliatelle and stir through, then cook for 1–2 minutes. Using a spaghetti spoon, transfer the pasta straight into the baking dish, dragging a little of the cooking water with it, and toss well. Tear the burrata over the top and finish with a drizzle of olive oil, a grinding of pepper and a scattering of extra basil leaves.

Hand-cut sagne a pezze WITH SLOW-cooked lamb ragù

This sauce is a classic from my Nonna Irene, whose Abruzzese heritage meant she knew a thing or two about cooking tender lamb. You will notice that there are no herbs or other extraneous flavours in the sauce, apart from garlic and a small piece of capsicum. This is the way my nonna taught me and it's how I like to reproduce it, to honour her culinary legacy and that of many Abruzzese women of her time, who never went down the route of 'fancy' cooking and trusted that a few key ingredients were enough to create a spectacular sauce. They were so right.

The name of the pasta itself means 'torn-up pasta sheet' in the Abruzzese dialect, and they are similar in size and shape to maltagliati. Even though my nonna was not terribly precise in the kitchen, she never tore the pasta; she always cut it into neat rectangles.

3 tablespoons extra-virgin olive oil
3 garlic cloves, bashed with the back of a knife
6 forequarter lamb chops (about 600 g in total)
200 ml red wine
2 x 400 g cans chopped tomatoes
¼ red capsicum, deseeded
salt flakes and freshly ground black pepper
1 quantity Whole-egg Pasta Dough (see page 20)
plain flour or coarse semolina, for dusting
freshly grated pecorino, to serve

SERVES 4–6

Heat the olive oil in a large heavy-based saucepan over medium heat, add the garlic and cook for 2–3 minutes until fragrant. Add the lamb chops and brown all over. Pour in the red wine and cook over high heat for 2 minutes or until reduced slightly, stirring to scrape up any caramelised bits caught on the base.

Add the tomatoes, then fill each empty can with water and pour them into the saucepan. Add the piece of capsicum and bring to a simmer, then reduce the heat to low, cover and simmer gently for 3–4 hours or until the meat falls off the bone. Nonna would lift out the meat and reserve it for another meal. You can do that if you like, or remove it from the pan and shred the meat, discarding any bones, then stir it back into the sauce. You can either leave the piece of capsicum in there or remove it – it is simply there to impart extra flavour. Season to taste.

While the ragù is cooking, make the pasta dough as instructed. After it has rested it will feel elastic and very pliable. Dust your board with flour or coarse semolina, and roll the dough into a 3–4 mm thick square or rectangle. Dust the rolled dough with extra flour or semolina, then cut it into 3 cm x 2 cm rectangles. Dust again and set aside.

Bring a large saucepan of salted water to the boil, drop in the pasta and stir through, then cook for 1–2 minutes. Using a spaghetti spoon, transfer the pasta straight into the ragù, dragging a little of the cooking water with it, and toss well. Top with freshly grated pecorino and serve.

Fresh egg SPAGHETTI WITH roasted LEMON AND scampi

It is no secret that Italian cooks favour olive oil, but I do like to sneak in a little butter when I make this zesty scampi sauce. Somehow its creaminess seems to enhance the natural juiciness of the blushing scampi. The slightly bitter tang of the roasted lemon juice perfectly offsets the richness, creating a dish that is impressive and complex in flavour, but quite easy to make.

1 quantity Whole-egg Pasta Dough (see page 20)
plain flour and coarse semolina, for dusting
2 lemons, halved
80 ml (⅓ cup) extra-virgin olive oil
20 g butter
1 garlic clove, finely chopped
1 tablespoon finely chopped flat-leaf parsley stalks
8 scampi, halved lengthways
finely grated zest of 1 lemon

SERVES 4

Make the pasta dough as instructed. After it has rested it will feel elastic and very pliable. Dust your board with flour or coarse semolina, and cut the dough into quarters. Work with one piece at a time and keep the rest wrapped up to prevent the dough from drying out. Flatten the dough with the palm of your hand, then pass it through the pasta machine's widest setting three or four times, folding the dough into three each time. Continue passing the dough through the machine (no further folding required), each time through a thinner setting, until you get to the second-last setting or the sheet is roughly 2.5 mm thick.

At this point, pass the dough sheet through the spaghetti cutter. Gently place the cut noodles on a floured tea towel, dust with semolina and allow to dry slightly at room temperature. Repeat with the remaining portions of dough.

Meanwhile, preheat your oven to 180°C and line a baking tray with baking paper.

Place the lemon on the prepared tray, drizzle with 1–2 tablespoons of the olive oil and roast for 20–25 minutes or until slightly caramelised. Some of the juices will have dripped onto the baking paper and turned nutty brown. Dip the cut sides of the lemon halves into that pool, then squeeze the juice into a bowl and reserve for later.

Bring a large saucepan of salted water to the boil.

In the meantime, melt the butter and remaining olive oil in a large frying pan over medium heat, add the garlic and parsley stalks, then the scampi and toss well to prevent the garlic from burning. Add the reserved lemon juice and cook for 1–2 minutes, then turn off the heat.

Drop the spaghetti into the boiling water and stir through, then cook for 2 minutes. Using a spaghetti spoon, transfer the spaghetti straight into the sauce, dragging a little of the cooking water with it. Place the pan over medium heat and stir for 1–2 minutes until creamy (add some of the pasta cooking water if it looks like it's drying out). Sprinkle with the lemon zest and serve.

Fresh spaghetti AL SUGO

I couldn't possibly list my top pasta dishes without giving a special mention to pasta al sugo, a meal Italians eat almost every day. Sugo is Italian for tomato sauce, which is made simply with olive oil, a little garlic or onion (sometimes both) and passata, simmered to create a thick coating for our pasta of choice. Sugo is the first sauce we ever learn to make and one we return to again and again. It is often the base for other dishes, like pasta bakes (see page 66).

Of course you don't have to make your own pasta if that sounds too daunting. It's easy to buy good-quality fresh pasta these days, which I do whenever I run out of my homemade stash.

1 quantity Whole-egg Pasta Dough (see page 20)
plain flour and coarse semolina, for dusting

SUGO
2 tablespoons extra-virgin olive oil
1 golden shallot, finely chopped
1 garlic clove, bashed with the back of a knife (or finely chopped, if you like a more pungent aroma)
400 g can peeled tomatoes or 400 ml Quick and Easy Passata (see opposite)
salt flakes

TO SERVE
freshly grated parmigiano
basil leaves
freshly ground black pepper

SERVES 4

Make the pasta dough as instructed. After it has rested it will feel elastic and very pliable. Dust your board with flour or coarse semolina, and cut the dough into quarters. Work with one piece at a time and keep the rest wrapped up to prevent the dough from drying out. Flatten the dough with the palm of your hand, then pass it through the pasta machine's widest setting three or four times, folding the dough into three each time. Continue passing the dough through the machine (no further folding required), each time through a thinner setting, until you get to the second-last setting or the sheet is roughly 2.5 mm thick.

At this point, pass the dough sheet through the spaghetti cutter. Gently place the cut noodles on a floured tea towel, dust with semolina and allow to dry slightly at room temperature. Repeat with the remaining portions of dough.

To make the sugo, heat the olive oil in a large frying pan over medium heat, add the shallot and garlic and cook for 1 minute or until fragrant (watch it closely as the garlic can burn very quickly). Add the tomatoes or passata and season with salt, then reduce the heat to low and simmer for 30 minutes or until slightly reduced. If it looks too dry you can add a little water.

Bring a large saucepan of salted water to the boil, drop in the spaghetti and stir through, then cook for 1–2 minutes. Using a spaghetti spoon, transfer the pasta straight into the sugo, dragging a little of the cooking water with it, and toss well over medium heat for 20–30 seconds. Finish with a generous dusting of parmigiano, some basil leaves and a good grinding of pepper.

Quick AND EASY passata

I was introduced to the delicate sweetness of homemade passata at a very early age. Every August, we children were assigned the task of washing piles of plump tomatoes, so ripe they almost burst in our tiny and clumsy hands. Mamma and Nonna would put them in a cauldron with a few other essential ingredients and leave them to stew gently, giving off a sweet smell that infused the kitchen walls, our clothes and our hair. They would then mill them vigorously to make a thick crimson nectar, ready to be bottled. All of a sudden the prospect of a long, cold Italian winter seemed more manageable!

3 kg ripe tomatoes, quartered
2 celery stalks, roughly chopped
2 spring onions, roughly chopped
1 red chilli (leave this out if you don't like heat)
2 large handfuls of basil leaves
a few oregano sprigs
salt flakes

MAKES 5 × 450 G JARS

Put all the ingredients except the salt in a large saucepan. Bring to a simmer over medium heat, then reduce the heat to low and cook gently for 35–40 minutes or until the vegetables have softened and your home is infused with the scent of Italy. Taste and season with salt to your liking.

Allow to cool in the pan for 10 minutes, then, working in batches, pass the mixture through a food mill. You could also pass it through a sieve or muslin cloth to get rid of the tomato seeds, but I like mine rustic and a little bit chunky.

Pour the passata back into the saucepan and warm for a few minutes over medium heat. Stir through more salt to taste, then pour the hot sauce into freshly sterilised glass jars (see notes).

Store the jars in a dark cupboard and consume within 6 months. Once opened, store in the fridge for up to 3 days. Summer in a bottle!

NOTES

To sterilise your jars, wash the jars and lids in hot soapy water, rinse and place on a tray in a 150°C oven for 10–15 minutes. Alternatively, you can place your washed and rinsed jars and lids in a large stockpot, cover with water and boil them for 20 minutes.

You can double, triple or quadruple this recipe to suit your needs.

Always use new lids for your jars to ensure that they seal properly.

Roasted PUMPKIN, cinnamon AND amaretti TORTELLI

This pumpkin tortelli has been on my family's Christmas Eve table for as long as I can remember. It's a beautiful tribute to my paternal nonna Pina, who was from Emilia-Romagna, the land of ravioli. Pumpkin is at its seasonal best in Italy at Christmas time and pairs so well with a hint of cinnamon and the bittersweet crunch of amaretti crumbs. Of course, you don't have to wait until the silly season to create this show stopper, especially given that the pumpkin season down under is during May and June! Any special occasion will do. The labour-intensive nature of this dish calls for some extra hands: you could ask your friends and family to create a production line to help fill and shape these delectable nuggets. Pasta party, anyone?

1 quantity Whole-egg Pasta Dough (see page 20)
plain flour and coarse semolina, for dusting

FILLING
700 g pumpkin (any kind), skin on, deseeded and cut into chunks
80 ml (⅓ cup) extra-virgin olive oil
2 tablespoons balsamic vinegar
1 teaspoon ground cinnamon, plus extra to taste
salt flakes and freshly ground black pepper
2 garlic cloves, skin on
2–3 sage leaves, or to taste
125 g (1¼ cups) dried breadcrumbs
50 g (½ cup) freshly grated parmigiano
30 g crushed amaretti cookies (see note)

SAUCE
120 g butter
8–10 sage leaves
pinch of salt flakes
freshly ground black pepper

SERVES 4–6

Preheat your oven to 200°C and line a baking tray with baking paper.

To make the filling, place the pumpkin on the prepared tray, add the olive oil, vinegar, cinnamon and some salt and pepper and toss to coat. Scatter over the garlic and sage leaves and roast for 45–50 minutes or until the pumpkin is soft. Discard the sage, remove the pumpkin skin and squeeze the garlic out of its skin. Mash the pumpkin and garlic with a fork until smooth. Add the breadcrumbs, parmigiano and three-quarters of the amaretti, then taste for seasoning and adjust. At this point I add a little more cinnamon, but you may choose not to. Place in the fridge until cool. You can make the filling up to 2 days ahead and keep it in the fridge.

Make the pasta dough as instructed. After it has rested it will feel elastic and pliable. Dust your board with flour or semolina, and cut the dough into quarters. Work with one piece at a time and keep the rest wrapped up to prevent it from drying out. Flatten the dough with the palm of your hand, then pass it through the pasta machine's widest setting three or four times, folding the dough into three each time. Continue passing the dough through the machine (no further folding required), each time through a thinner setting, until you get to the second-last setting or the sheet is roughly 2.5 mm thick.

Dust your work surface with semolina. Lay the long sheet of pasta out flat, then evenly dot heaped teaspoons of the filling down one side, leaving about 3 cm between each dollop. Brush around the filling with water to moisten, then fold the sheet over and press down to seal. Gently press around each mound to remove any air bubbles (otherwise the tortelli may burst when you cook them). Cut into 4 cm squares with a pastry wheel, then place the tortelli on a platter dusted with semolina, trying not to overlap them. Repeat with the remaining dough and filling. You can cook the tortelli straight away or freeze them for up to 2 weeks.

Bring a large saucepan of salted water to the boil.   >

Meanwhile, to make the sauce, place the butter, sage and salt in a large heavy-based frying pan over medium heat and cook until the butter is a pale caramel colour and the sage leaves are crispy.

Add the tortelli to the boiling water and cook for 2–3 minutes. Using a slotted spoon, lift them from the water and drop them into the brown butter sauce. Saute for 2–3 minutes or until all the tortelli are nicely coated and slightly caramelised. Season with pepper.

Arrange the tortelli on a large serving platter and top with the fried sage leaves and remaining crushed amaretti. Serve hot!

NOTE
Amaretti cookies are golden brown with a hard texture and you can find them at most delis. To crush them, either blitz them in a food processor or cut them with a knife – they crumble quite easily.

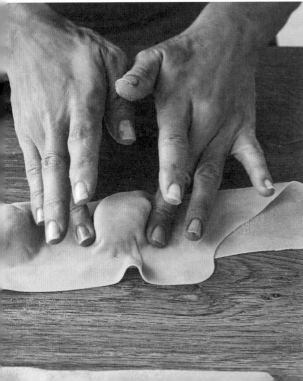

HAND-CUT *spelt* pappardelle WITH *slow-* cooked pork ragù

Hand-rolling and cutting fresh pasta might sound laborious, but if the dough is well rested it takes very little time and the effort involved repays you tenfold in texture. And if, like me, you are not bound by the rules of strict precision, your hand-cut noodles will be a little unruly and have their own personality, which you will fully appreciate when they end up in your mouth!

When making a pork ragù I like to use shoulder as it becomes beautifully soft after a long, slow simmer, and is easily shredded with a fork. My mamma and my nonna would actually remove the pork and save it for another meal, and simply coat the pasta with the rich pork-infused sauce. This is very common in Italian home cooking as we like to cook once and eat twice where possible. Whichever way you serve this, I'm am sure you will love it!

300 g (2 cups) plain or
    type '00' flour
100 g spelt flour
4 eggs, at room temperature
1 scant teaspoon salt flakes
plain flour or coarse semolina,
    for dusting
freshly grated pecorino, to serve

PORK RAGÙ
100 ml extra-virgin olive oil
3 garlic cloves, skin on, bashed
    with the back of a knife
500 g piece of boneless pork
    shoulder
1 onion, chopped
1 carrot, chopped
1 celery stalk, chopped
1 teaspoon fennel seeds
2–3 juniper berries, lightly
    crushed with a mortar and
    pestle or rolling pin
4–5 marjoram leaves
200 ml red wine
400 g can chopped tomatoes
500 ml (2 cups) good-quality
    beef or chicken stock
3–4 sage leaves
salt flakes and freshly ground
    white pepper

SERVES 4

To make the pork ragù, heat 3 tablespoons of the olive oil in a large heavy-based saucepan over high heat, add the garlic and cook, stirring, for 1 minute, then add the pork and brown all over for 2–3 minutes. Remove the pork and set aside. Pour the remaining oil into the pan and reduce the heat to medium. Add the onion, carrot, celery, fennel seeds, juniper berries and marjoram and cook, stirring, for a few minutes until the onion is soft and translucent.

Return the pork to the pan and cook over high heat for 2 minutes, then deglaze the pan with the wine, scraping up any bits caught on the base. Simmer for 2 minutes until the alcohol has evaporated. Add the tomatoes and stock, bring to a simmer, then reduce the heat to low. Add the sage and season with salt, then cover and cook for 3–4 hours, stirring occasionally. Add a splash of water If It starts to dry out.

Towards the end of the cooking time, taste for salt and adjust if needed, then season with white pepper. Discard the garlic cloves. Remove the pork and shred using a fork, then return it to the sauce or keep it for another meal.

When the sauce is nearly ready, place the flours on a board, make a well in the centre and drop in the eggs and salt. Combine using your fingers or a fork, then knead the mixture vigorously for about 10 minutes. At first it will look crumbly, but once your body heat activates the starch in the flour the dough will change in texture, turning into a smooth, firm ball. If you think it looks too dry (sometimes spelt flour can do that), gradually add up to 1 tablespoon of water and knead until smooth. Wrap it (I use beeswax wraps) and let it rest at room temperature for 20 minutes.

After the dough has rested it will feel elastic and very pliable. Dust your board with flour or semolina and roll the dough into a 3–4 mm thick disc. Dust with extra flour or semolina, then roll it up into a log. Using a sharp knife, cut the log into 2 cm thick slices. Use your fingers to unravel the slices into long pasta ribbons and dust with more flour or semolina.   >

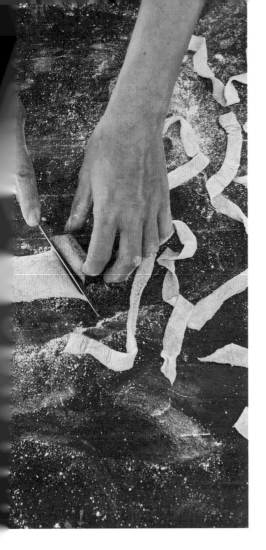

Bring a large saucepan of salted water to the boil, drop in the pappardelle and cook for 2 minutes. Drain well, but be sure to reserve a couple of tablespoons of the pasta cooking water to add to the ragù. This will help bind the sauce and create a richer, creamier texture.

Add the pappardelle and reserved water to the ragù and toss to combine. Serve dusted with pecorino and a little extra white pepper.

BASIC VEGAN pasta dough

Have you ever tasted homemade orecchiette in Puglia? Or vacationed in Tuscany and eaten forkfuls of fat homemade spaghetti called pici? I bet you didn't know that those traditional pasta shapes are made with just flour, water and a pinch of salt. In fact, many pastas are eggless, from well-known dried varieties (linguine, rigatoni, penne and the like) to regional specialities, such as strozzapreti, scialatielli or the intricate Sardinian lorighittas.

Some recipes call for 100% durum wheat flour, a fine semolina flour primarily used for pasta making. I find that a dough solely made of semolina can be very hard to roll and I prefer cutting it with type '00' flour to give it more pliability. I recommend trying both ways and seeing which one you prefer.

150 g (1 cup) type '00' or specialty pasta flour, plus extra for dusting
150 g semolina flour (see note), plus extra for dusting
1 teaspoon salt flakes
250 ml (1 cup) lukewarm water

SERVES 4

Put the flours and salt in a large mixing bowl, make a well in the centre and slowly start pouring in the water, mixing as you go to incorporate the flour. Don't add all the water at once as you may not need it all.

Tip the dough onto a floured surface, oil your hands and knead for 3–4 minutes or until it comes together in a smooth ball. Add a little extra flour if the dough feels a bit wet.

Wrap it in plastic wrap or a beeswax wrap and let it rest at room temperature for 30 minutes.

NOTE
Semolina flour (or semola) is fine durum wheat flour and is sold in specialty stores or online.

Homemade TROFIE with pesto alla GENOVEASE

Turning emerald-green basil into Italy's most-loved pasta condiment is an easy task, but it takes love and a commitment to authenticity to make a really good pesto. The name of this ancient Ligurian dish comes from the method used to produced it: in the Genovese dialect the word pestâ (pestare in Italian) means to pound or to crush, in this case with a marble mortar and pestle. These days it's quite acceptable to use a food processor. I'm sharing a more traditional version of the recipe, including boiled potato and green beans, which elevate it to a delectable, substantial meal. It is usually served with trofie, a curly short pasta from Liguria.

1 quantity Basic Vegan Pasta Dough (see opposite)
coarse semolina or semolina flour (see note opposite), for dusting
1 potato, peeled and cut into small cubes
150 g green beans, trimmed and cut into thirds
baby basil leaves, to serve (optional)

PESTO GENOVESE
2 large bunches of basil, stalks trimmed
2 ice cubes (see notes)
1 garlic clove, peeled
50 g (⅓ cup) pine nuts
3 tablespoons freshly grated parmigiano
3 tablespoons freshly grated pecorino
180 ml (¾ cup) extra-virgin olive oil
salt flakes

SERVES 4

Make the pasta dough as instructed. After it has rested, dust a large board or surface with semolina. Pinch off a 2 cm piece of the dough. Use the palm of your hand to roll it out on the board, then, using the side of your hand, drag it diagonally towards you to create a spiral (the dough will stretch to be about ½ cm thick). Repeat with the remaining dough. Dust the trofie with semolina and set aside.

Next, make your pesto.

If you are using a food processor, put the basil, ice cubes, garlic, pine nuts and cheese in a food processor and blitz until smooth. Slowly add the olive oil in a thin stream and process until dense and well emulsified. Season to taste with salt.

If you are using a mortar and pestle, place the basil, garlic, pine nuts and a pinch of salt in the mortar. Start working with the pestle, pressing and rotating it until all the ingredients are nicely ground. Add the cheese and mix well. Slowly pour in the olive oil and mix until well emulsified. Season to taste with salt.

Place the pesto in the fridge until needed (it will keep, well covered in olive oil, for more than a week). This is a double batch, because why not? You can store the leftover pesto in the fridge or freezer for later use.

When you are ready to cook, spoon half the pesto into a large serving bowl.

Bring a large saucepan of salted water to the boil. Drop in the potato and cook for 8–10 minutes or until almost cooked through. Add the trofie and beans and cook for 2–3 minutes. Use a slotted spoon to lift the trofie, potato and beans straight into the serving bowl, dragging along a little of the pasta cooking water, and mix thoroughly with the pesto. Top with some basil, if you like, and serve hot!

NOTES
The ice cubes help preserve the vibrant green hue of the basil if you are using a food processor for the pesto. Leave them out if you are making it with a mortar and pestle.

Authentic pesto is not garlic loaded but you can add more garlic if you like it very pungent.

TUSCAN pici in a FRESH tomato AND garlic SAUCE

It is almost impossible to travel around Tuscany and not encounter this plate of pasta – one of the region's signature dishes – which goes by the name of pici all'aglione. Its beauty lies in its utter simplicity: silky, chubby strands of homemade pasta lusciously coated in a rich tomato and garlic sauce. Just add parmigiano and a glass of Chianti!

1 quantity Basic Vegan Pasta Dough (see page 38)
coarse semolina or semolina flour (see note page 38), for dusting
800 g roma tomatoes
iced water, for refreshing
80 ml (⅓ cup) extra-virgin olive oil
3 garlic cloves, thinly sliced
a few rosemary sprigs
salt flakes and freshly ground black pepper
freshly grated parmigiano, to serve (optional)

SERVES 4

Make the pasta dough as instructed. After it has rested, pinch small pieces of dough (about the size of a small walnut) and roll with your hands into 5 mm thick lengths. If need be, oil your hands with a little olive oil to help with the shaping process. Dust the rolled dough with semolina and set aside.

Score the top of the tomatoes with a sharp knife. Bring a large saucepan of salted water to the boil, drop in the tomatoes and blanch for about 1–2 minutes. Lift them out with a slotted spoon, reserving the cooking liquid, and place in a bowl of iced water to arrest the cooking. Remove the skins (you will find they come off really easily), then drain the tomatoes and crush them with a fork or a potato masher. Some people like to remove the seeds, but I leave them in for a more rustic texture.

Heat the olive oil in a large frying pan over medium heat, add the garlic and cook for 1 minute or until fragrant (watch closely as garlic can burn very quickly!). Drop in the crushed tomato and rosemary sprigs and season with salt and pepper. Reduce the heat to low and simmer for 30 minutes or until slightly reduced. If it looks too dry add a little of the tomato blanching water.

Bring the tomato blanching water back to the boil, drop in the pici and stir well to prevent them from sticking. Cook for 3–4 minutes (you will find that eggless pasta needs 1–2 minutes more than pasta made with egg). Use a spaghetti spoon to lift the pici straight into the sauce, dragging a little of the cooking water with it, then toss well over medium heat for 20–30 seconds to combine. Serve hot with some grated parmigiano scattered over the top, if you like.

BUSIATE ALLA Trapanese

In Italy pesto refers to any sauce that's 'pestata' (ground together with a mortar and pestle). Everybody knows and loves pesto Genovese (see page 39), but the Sicilian town of Trapani is also renowned for a pesto recipe that combines nuts and herbs with two other iconic Italian ingredients: ricotta and tomatoes. The results are sensational and if, like me, you make this in the food processor, your next meal is only 10 minutes away. Traditionally, pesto Trapanese is served with busiate, a curly handmade Sicilian pasta, but if you are not feeling that adventurous, don't despair – this sauce is fantastic with linguine, rigatoni or even casarecce and orecchiette. If you do want to give it a try, you'll need a knitting needle or a chopstick to help shape the pasta.

1 quantity Basic Vegan Pasta Dough (see page 38)
coarse semolina or semolina flour (see note page 38), for dusting
basil leaves, to serve (optional)
3 tablespoons toasted almond flakes (optional)

PESTO TRAPANESE
70 g blanched almonds
½ garlic clove
80 g (¾ cup) freshly grated parmigiano
150 g fresh ricotta
4–5 semi-dried tomatoes
500 g truss tomatoes, roughly chopped
1 large bunch of basil, stalks trimmed
salt flakes and freshly ground black pepper

SERVES 4

Make the pasta dough as instructed. After it has rested, dust a large board or surface with semolina. Roll the dough into 1 cm thick ropes, then cut it into 1 cm pieces. Take one piece at a time and roll it with your hands into a very thin rope. Cut the rope in half and roll each piece around a chopstick or knitting needle, then gently ease it out to reveal its curly look. Repeat with the remaining dough. Dust the rolled dough with semolina and set aside.

To make the pesto Trapanese, place the almonds, garlic and parmigiano in a food processor and whiz until it resembles sand. Add the remaining ingredients and process for 30 seconds or until combined but not perfectly smooth – a little texture is welcome here. Taste and adjust the seasoning if necessary.

Spoon the pesto into a large serving bowl.

Bring a large saucepan of salted water to the boil. Drop in the busiate and cook for 3–4 minutes. Use a slotted spoon to lift the pasta straight into the serving bowl, dragging along a little of the pasta cooking water, and mix thoroughly with the pesto. Serve as is, or top with some basil leaves and toasted almond flakes, if you like.

HOMEMADE cavatelli WITH spring VEGETABLES

Shaping cavatelli is one of my favourite stress-relieving activities. Once I have rested my dough and dusted my board, I immerse myself in the repetitive pinching, rolling and dragging action. I'm never fussed if they are not particularly precise – all I really care about is creating a slit in the middle big enough to trap the goodness of the sauce. The name cavetelli comes from the word 'cavati' (hollow), which is what makes this shape so efficient and so satisfying to the palate.

1 quantity Basic Vegan Pasta Dough (see page 38)
coarse semolina or semolina flour (see note page 38), for dusting
1 bunch of asparagus, woody ends trimmed
iced water, for refreshing
4 baby zucchini with their flowers attached
3 tablespoons extra-virgin olive oil
2 golden shallots, thinly sliced
1 garlic clove, skin on, bashed with the back of a knife
salt flakes and freshly ground black pepper
3 tablespoons frozen peas

TO SERVE
finely grated lemon zest
baby mint leaves (optional)
freshly grated pecorino (optional)

SERVES 4

Make the pasta dough as instructed. After it has rested, dust a large board or surface with semolina. Pinch off a 2 cm piece of dough, then use a butter knife to drag it towards you – the dough will stretch out and an indent will be created in the middle. Repeat with the remaining dough. Dust the cavatelli with semolina and set aside.

Cut the asparagus spears into three or four pieces, depending on their size. If the spears are very big, you might like to peel them to remove the stringy outer layer. Leave the tips intact.

Bring a large saucepan of salted water to the boil. Drop in the asparagus and blanch for 2 minutes. Use a slotted spoon to lift them out and plunge them into iced water, then drain and set aside. Reserve the boiling water as you will use it to cook your cavatelli.

Separate the baby zucchini from their flowers. Remove the stamen within the petals, then open them and shred the flowers. Slice the baby zucchini into thin rounds.

Heat the olive oil in a large heavy-based frying pan over medium heat, add the shallot, garlic and a pinch of salt and saute for 2–3 minutes. Add the zucchini rounds and cook for another 2–3 minutes until they start to colour. Add the peas and asparagus and cook for 1–2 minutes. Remove from the heat, then discard the garlic clove and season to taste with salt and pepper.

Bring the saucepan of water back to the boil, drop in your cavatelli and boil for 3–4 minutes or until cooked.

While the cavatelli is cooking, return the frying pan with the vegetable mixture to medium heat. Use a slotted spoon to lift the cavatelli out of the cooking water and straight into the pan, dragging a little of the cooking water with it, and saute briefly to lightly colour and mingle with the greens. Add a little more cooking water if it seems a bit dry. Scatter over the lemon zest and shredded zucchini flowers, then top with some mint leaves and grated pecorino, if you like, and serve.

Dried
PASTA

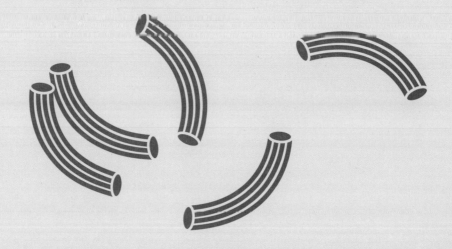

When I first moved to Australia I was really surprised to learn that dried pasta was considered to be cheat's pasta. Trust this Italian lady: if you are using pasta from a packet, you are not cheating; you are channelling what most Italians do most days. Dried pasta is not just convenient, it's also delicious and it is only with dried pasta that you can achieve that highly coveted al dente texture (see page 16). Dried pasta is made with durum wheat flour and water, extruded through specially crafted machines into various shapes, then left to dry for days. Italians are extremely proud of it. We like to think that there is no dried pasta quite like the ones made on our soil, with our wonderful wheat, perfect water and temperate climate. This is the kind of pasta that will keep its texture when cooked and give you that wonderful toothy feel as you bite it. We are so completely obsessed with it that we often have it dressed with just a lick of olive oil and a dusting of parmigiano, to fully appreciate its natural flavour.

Another merit of dried pasta is that it comes in myriad shapes, each designed to serve a specific purpose. For example, spaghetti and linguine are often paired with shellfish, particularly clams and mussels. In fact, I challenge you to find a restaurant in Italy that will serve anything other than spaghetti or linguine with vongole. As always, there are exceptions to this rule, namely paccheri, a short pasta that looks like massive rigatoni, and conchiglie, a shell-shaped pasta, both of which pair beautifully with seafood. Interestingly, if you use fresh tagliatelle or pappardelle with your vongole sauce you will find that it dries out a little, as fresh pasta tends to absorb more liquid, and the temptation would be to add more oil, butter or, God forbid, cream!

You might be surprised to know that Italians never match spaghetti with bolognese sauce. It's only ever served with fresh tagliatelle, as its soft texture marries beautifully with the richness of the sauce. Having said that, please don't feel that you can never enjoy a bowl of spag bol again. Have it with whatever pasta is in easy reach to make your family dinner a happy and stress-free one. Just be aware that you will never see this combination on a menu in Italy.

Short pasta shapes, such as orecchiette, rigatoni, penne and fusilli, are made to capture chunky sauces in their sturdy hollows and ridges, giving satisfying bursts of flavour as you eat. They are very versatile and larger varieties are wonderfully suited to pasta bakes.

There is one short pasta shape that tends to cause controversy in my house: penne! They come in two varieties – liscie (smooth) and rigate (with ridges) – and the choice is completely personal. And while I do appreciate the great flavour offered by the rigate type, and the way the sauce clings so well to its surface, my Nonno Domenico and I have always shared a preference for liscie. Go team liscie!

Note: If you follow a gluten-free diet, rest assured that exceptional gluten-free dried pastas are now readily available. All the sauces in this chapter will work beautifully with gluten-free pasta.

Spaghetti ALLA CARBONARA

Carbonara is said to have been created by the Carbonari, groups of secret revolutionary societies founded in the early 19th century who sought the creation of a liberal, unified Italy. Others say that it was first invented by some Italian charcoal burners, also called carbonari. One thing we do know for sure is that carbonara is an incredibly delicious sauce made with just four ingredients: eggs, pork, black pepper and pecorino. Because of the recipe's simplicity, (non-Italian) home cooks and chefs are often tempted to add extraneous ingredients, such as garlic, onion, parsley or, any Italian's worst fear, cream! Please don't do this! The Carbonari knew what they were doing back in 1820, and in Italy the dish has remained unchanged to this day. It is perfect as it is.

To summarise, here is a little carbonara rule book I swear by:

1. Absolutely, unequivocally NO cream needed.
2. If you can't find guanciale (cured pork jowl), smoked pancetta is also acceptable.
3. Vegan carbonara doesn't exist. Sorry (not sorry), but when a sauce is made with four ingredients, three of which are eggs, cheese and meat, and you use vegan-friendly substitutes, then carbonara it ain't.

Sticking to tradition is one of the few ways we have to preserve and honour our past. Think of it as an act of respect for those who came before us!

400 g dried spaghetti
1 tablespoon extra-virgin olive oil
150 g (½ cup) diced guanciale
3 egg yolks
1 teaspoon salt flakes
1 tablespoon freshly ground black pepper, plus extra to serve (optional)
100 g (1 cup) freshly grated pecorino, plus extra to serve

SERVES 4

Bring a large saucepan of salted water to the boil. Drop in the spaghetti and stir to separate the strands, then cook for 1–2 minutes or until nicely al dente.

While your spaghetti is cooking, heat the olive oil in a large frying pan over low heat. Add the guanciale and gently fry until it renders its fat and turns crispy and pink.

Beat the eggs yolks, salt and pepper in a small bowl. Add the pecorino and beat well to combine.

Using a spaghetti spoon, transfer the spaghetti straight into the pan, dragging a little of the cooking water with it, and toss with the guanciale to allow the flavours to combine. Reserve a few tablespoons of the pasta cooking water.

Take the pan off the heat, add the egg and cheese mixture and stir through very quickly to avoid overcooking the egg, adding a little of the reserved pasta cooking water if it looks a bit dry. Add a little more cheese to bring the temperature down and amalgamate. The residual heat of the pan, spaghetti and cooking water will gently cook the egg, but keep it nice and creamy. Grind over a bit more pepper if you like and serve straight away.

Ziti rotti
WITH RAGÙ
Genovese

This traditional Italian dish dates back to the 15th century and is a signature dish of Cucina Napoletana. The name 'Genovese' suggests its birth place should be Genova, however it's more likely it was first made by someone whose surname was 'il Genovese' (the one from Genova) and the name stuck. Unlike most Italian meat-based pasta sauces, ragù Genovese is made without tomatoes. Plenty of onions and olive oil create the base, and the sauce needs to stew for hours until the onion is jammy and the meat is fall-apart tender.

When it comes to the type of pasta to accompany it, the Neapolitans stand firm: it must be ziti, a long tubular pasta that is broken by hand ('rotti' means broken) before cooking. This is the only time Italians agree to break long pasta before cooking. Never try this with linguine or spaghetti in front of an Italian if you value your life! If ziti are hard to come by, paccheri or rigatoni are the only acceptable substitutes.

This sauce needs time to develop so make it the day before you want to eat it.

2½ tablespoons extra-virgin
   olive oil
3 small onions, finely chopped
1 carrot, finely chopped
1 celery stalk, finely chopped
300 g chuck steak, cut into
   large chunks
300 g beef cheeks, cut into
   large chunks
200 ml white wine
salt flakes and freshly ground
   black pepper
400 g dried ziti pasta
freshly grated parmigiano,
   to serve

SERVES 4–6

Heat the olive oil in a large heavy-based saucepan over medium heat, add the onion, carrot and celery and cook until softened. Add the meat (in batches if needed so you don't overcrowd the pan) and brown well all over. Deglaze the pan with the wine, scraping up any bits caught on the base, and cook out the alcohol for 3–4 minutes.

Add 800 ml of water and season to taste (don't over-season at this point as the long, slow cooking process will intensify the flavours). Cover and cook over low heat for 4–6 hours (or even 8 hours, if you can!). You'll know it's ready when the meat falls apart and the sauce is dark and has left a coating on the side of the pan. Leave it in the pan and place in the fridge overnight to allow the flavours to develop.

When you are ready to eat, bring a large saucepan of salted water to the boil. Break the ziti in half with your hands, drop them into the pan and stir well, then cook for 8 minutes or until al dente.

Meanwhile, heat up the sauce, breaking up the meat with a fork if you need to. Use a slotted spoon to transfer the ziti to a large serving platter, dragging along a little pasta cooking water, then top with the ragù and toss well. Make sure the ziti are perfectly coated in the sauce. Finish with a sprinkling of parmigiano and serve hot.

Rigatoni ALLA GRICIA

This once little-known Roman dish has risen to fame in the last few years. Gricia seems to be following the same trajectory as the ubiquitous cacio e pepe, and is now proudly featured on restaurant menus around the globe. Like its famous cousin, gricia is a two-ingredient pasta sauce: guanciale (cured pork jowl) and pecorino. Any additions, substitutions or alterations will not be tolerated by Italians (please refer to my earlier rant about carbonara on page 52). However, we are more lenient when it comes to the choice of pasta: rigatoni, mezze maniche or even bucatini and spaghetti all have the stamp of approval from traditional Roman trattorias, so use what you have. And of course, a little black pepper is always welcome.

400 g dried rigatoni
3 tablespoons extra-virgin olive oil
150 g guanciale, cut into 4 mm wide strips
130 g pecorino, freshly grated
freshly ground black pepper

SERVES 4

Bring a large saucepan of salted water to the boil. Drop in the rigatoni and stir well, then cook for 8 minutes or until nicely al dente.

Meanwhile, heat the olive oil in a large frying pan over low heat, add the guanciale and fry gently for 5–6 minutes until the fat has rendered out and the guanciale is crispy.

Drain the pasta, reserving some of the starchy cooking water. Tip the pasta into the pan and toss well. Remove from the heat, add two-thirds of the cheese and a little pasta cooking water and stir vigorously to create a creamy texture.

Divide the pasta among bowls, top with the remaining cheese and a generous grinding of pepper and serve.

One-pot pasta done the Italian way!

Try to unsee all those videos circulating online showing uncooked onion, garlic (often garlic powder!), broken spaghetti, cheese and tomatoes thrown unceremoniously into a pan, stirred and cooked to oblivion. In Italy our method for making one-pot pasta is called 'pasta risottata' (cooked risotto style) and, unsurprisingly, the cooking technique bears many similarities to that of risotto. The garlic and onion are sauteed first, then the uncooked pasta is added, followed by just enough liquid to cover (either from tomatoes, passata, stock or water from a kettle). Both pasta and sauce cook at the same time and the end result is nothing short of spectacular. Occasional stirring while the pasta cooks releases enough starch to thicken the sauce and give it a lovely creamy consistency. And while it cooks, the pasta gradually absorbs the liquid, becoming infused with all the flavours in the pan. This amazing technique is not a trend – it's here to stay!

spaghetti ALLA puttanesca

This is one recipe I return to time and time again, partly because it is made entirely with pantry staples. And Nonna's little trick of adding an old pecorino or parmigiano rind elevates this evergreen to the next level. If you don't feel confident enough to whip this up in one pan, simply make the sauce, boil the pasta and then toss them together.

2 tablespoons extra-virgin olive oil
4–6 anchovy fillets
2–3 garlic cloves, skin on, bashed with the back of a knife
1 tablespoon finely chopped flat-leaf parsley stalks
400 g dried spaghetti
2–3 tablespoons capers, rinsed and drained
3 tablespoons pitted black olives
400 g can chopped tomatoes
small piece of pecorino or parmigiano rind (optional)
salt flakes and freshly ground black pepper (optional)
freshly grated pecorino or parmigiano, to serve
chopped flat-leaf parsley leaves, to serve

SERVES 4

Put the kettle on, as you will need to add boiling water to the pan when you add the pasta.

Heat the olive oil in a large heavy-based saucepan. Add the anchovy fillets and stir with a wooden spoon to break them down, then add the garlic and parsley stalks and stir to infuse the oil. Add the pasta, capers and olives and stir well.

Pour in the tomatoes and enough boiling water to cover all the pasta. Add your cheese rind, if using, and cook, stirring occasionally, for 7–8 minutes or until the pasta is al dente.

Discard the cheese rind and garlic, then taste and season with salt and pepper if needed (remember the capers, olives and anchovies are salty so don't overdo it). Finish with a sprinkling of grated cheese and chopped parsley and serve.

NOTE
Make sure you use a large pan so that your strands of spaghetti fit comfortably in one layer, without having to break them. If your pan isn't big enough, try using a different pasta shape, such as rigatone or penne.

Conchiglie WITH mussels, baby capers AND fresh TOMATOES

Conchiglie means 'seashells', so it is only fitting to pair this pasta shape with seafood. There is another reason I choose conchiglie when making this particular dish – they are quite small, which means that they fit perfectly in the pan, submerged in their cooking liquid, and the built-in hole mercilessly traps the sauce, giving it no chance to escape. However, in Italy the matter of conchiglie is not that simple as they come in three sizes: the large ones are generally filled for pasta bakes, while the baby ones are only used in soups, usually floating in a sea of homemade brodo (broth). For this dish you want the medium size, just big enough to take on the robust flavours of the mussels, capers and chilli.

8 roma tomatoes
iced water, for refreshing
80 ml (⅓ cup) extra-virgin olive oil
2 garlic cloves, skin on, bashed with the back of a knife
3 spring onions, sliced
½ long red chilli, thinly sliced, plus extra to serve
200 ml dry white wine
small handful of baby capers, rinsed and drained
1.5 kg fresh mussels, cleaned and debearded
350–400 g medium dried conchiglie pasta
handful of flat-leaf parsley leaves, roughly chopped (optional)
crusty bread, to serve

SERVES 4

Put the kettle on, as you will need to add boiling water to the pan when you add the pasta.

Score the top of the tomatoes with a sharp knife. Bring a large saucepan of salted water to the boil, drop in the tomatoes and blanch for about 1–2 minutes. Lift them out with a slotted spoon and place in a bowl of iced water to arrest the cooking. Remove the skins (you will find they come off really easily), then drain the tomatoes and roughly chop in a bowl so you save all the juices. Set aside.

Heat the olive oil in a large heavy-based saucepan over high heat. Add the garlic, spring onion and chilli and toss until the garlic starts to become golden and fragrant. Pour in the wine and cook for about 2 minutes until the alcohol has evaporated, then add the capers, chopped tomato and mussels. Cover with a tight-fitting lid and allow the mussels to steam. They will start to open after 1–2 minutes. As they do, lift them out with a slotted spoon and set them aside in a clean bowl. Discard any mussels that don't open.

Drop the pasta into the tomato sauce, then pour in enough boiling water to cover. Start stirring gently – the sauce will thicken ever so slightly as the conchiglie soak up all the juices. Cook for 8 minutes or until perfectly al dente. Remember, the residual heat will continue cooking the pasta when you turn off the heat, so it's a good idea to keep it very al dente.

Remove the pan from the heat and add the mussels, along with their precious resting juices, and toss everything together well. Scatter over the parsley (if using) and extra chilli and serve straight away with plenty of bread for mopping up the sauce.

NOTE
If you are pressed for time, you can use 200 ml of passata or 200 g of canned chopped tomatoes instead of the fresh roma tomatoes.

Casarecce with TUNA, capers AND bread-crumbs

This is an essential recipe that every Italian has up their sleeve. It's one of those dishes aptly named 'salva cena' (dinner saviour) as it can be made quickly using bits and pieces from your pantry – provided you have stocked it with Italian essentials. Even my Australian husband, after years of living with this hardcore Italian, knows better than to suggest takeaway on hump days, saying 'surely we (meaning me!) can whip up a pasta col tonno'.

2 tablespoons extra-virgin
    olive oil
2 spring onions, thinly sliced
1 garlic clove, thinly sliced
a few chillies (according to
    taste), sliced
300 g cherry tomatoes, halved
150 ml dry white wine
350–400 g dried casarecce
185 g can tuna in brine,
    well drained
2 tablespoons capers, rinsed
    and drained
3–4 tablespoons pitted
    black olives
salt flakes and freshly ground
    black pepper

BREADCRUMB TOPPING
2 tablespoons extra-virgin
    olive oil
60 g (¾ cup) fresh breadcrumbs
salt flakes
handful of chopped flat-leaf
    parsley leaves

SERVES 4

Put the kettle on, as you will need to add boiling water to the pan when you add the pasta.

To make the topping, heat the olive oil in a large heavy-based frying pan over medium–high heat. Add the breadcrumbs and cook, stirring, for 3–4 minutes until nicely golden and crunchy. Tip the crumbs onto a plate, season with a little salt and stir through the parsley. Set aside.

Wipe out the pan, add the olive oil and heat over medium–high heat. Add the spring onion, garlic, chilli and cherry tomatoes and cook for 1 minute. Deglaze the pan with the wine, scraping up any bits caught on the base, and cook out the alcohol for 1–2 minutes.

Add the casarecce, tuna, capers and olives and stir, then pour in enough boiling water to cover the pasta by 3–4 cm. Season with salt and cook, stirring occasionally, for 8 minutes or until the pasta is al dente. By now most of the liquid will have evaporated, creating a thick and luscious sauce. If it doesn't seem thick enough, turn up the heat during the last minute of cooking.

Season to taste with salt and pepper, then sprinkle over the breadcrumb topping and serve hot.

Baked
PASTA

Ask any Italian what they are having for Sunday lunch and the answer will usually be 'pasta al forno', a ritual that speaks of Italian gatherings like no other dish. No matter the occasion, or the season, a large tray of pasta will make its way into the oven, the heat melting the cheesy goodness within and creating coveted crunchy corners that Italians fight over. I'm calling it here – cook's privilege!

Literally meaning 'pasta in the oven', it's one of those dishes that will please everyone at the table, from children to grown-ups, fussy eaters to hungry ones. You can start easy by making a simple pasta with sugo (see pages 28 or 43), adding a little bit of mozzarella or provola and giving it enough time in a hot oven for the cheese to melt and develop a bronzed crust. Take it up a notch with some sausage meat rolled into meatballs and a few decadent dollops of bechamel (see page 68).

If you feel up for a challenge, take a bit more time and create a dish that will stop the whole family in their tracks. I'm talking about silky pasta filled with a delectable ricotta and spinach mixture and rolled into cannelloni; impressive timballo, festive enough to take centre stage at the Christmas table; and of course everybody's one true love: lasagne. I haven't included a recipe for classic lasagne here as I've already shared recipes in my previous books that I can't seem to beat. But don't despair – I am about to introduce you to a special type of lasagne you may not have encountered before. It is typical of the Abruzzo region, where my mamma comes from, using crespelle (crepes) instead of pasta sheets for the layers. Trust me, it is mind-blowingly good.

So crank up the oven and get baking!

Classic pasta al forno WITH sausage POLPETTE

Aside from its nostalgic appeal, pasta al forno is also an ingenious way to repurpose leftover pasta or sauce. Just add cheese and a white sauce! Short pasta shapes are always the favourite, especially rigatoni, but penne rigate or tortiglioni are also great. Basically anything short, tubular and with ridges is going to be your amico here. Italians never use spaghetti or any other long noodle for this dish, for no other reason than 'they are just wrong!'.

350 g dried rigatoni
small handful of freshly grated parmigiano or pecorino
100 g dry mozzarella (scamorza), sliced
basil leaves, to serve (optional)
freshly ground black pepper

PORK AND RED WINE SAUCE
500 g pork and fennel sausages
2 tablespoons extra-virgin olive oil
2 garlic cloves, bashed with the back of a knife
200 ml red wine
2 x 400 g cans chopped tomatoes
¼ red capsicum, deseeded
a few celery leaves
handful of flat-leaf parsley or basil leaves
salt flakes and freshly ground black pepper

BECHAMEL
60 g butter
3 tablespoons plain flour
500 ml (2 cups) milk
salt flakes and freshly ground black pepper
a little freshly grated nutmeg

SERVES 4

To make the pork and red wine sauce, remove the sausages from their casings and roll tablespoons of the meat into balls. Set aside.

Heat the olive oil in a frying pan over medium–high heat, add the garlic and let it infuse the oil. Add the meatballs and fry until browned all over. Deglaze the pan with the wine, scraping up any bits caught on the base, and cook off the alcohol (this should take 1–2 minutes). Add the tomatoes, then fill each empty can with water and pour them into the pan. Add the capsicum and celery leaves and bring to a simmer. Add the parsley or basil, then reduce the heat to low, cover and cook gently for 2 hours, stirring occasionally. Season to taste with salt and pepper.

Preheat your oven to 200°C.

To make the bechamel, melt the butter in a saucepan over medium heat, add the flour and whisk well. Cook for 2 minutes or until it comes away from the side of the pan, then gradually start adding the milk, stirring to eliminate any lumps. Season with salt, pepper and nutmeg. Bring to a simmer, stirring constantly, and cook over medium–low heat for 2–3 minutes or until thickened. Set aside.

Bring a large saucepan of salted water to the boil, add the rigatoni and cook until about three-quarters ready (it will finish cooking in the oven). Drain and toss in the tomato and meatball sauce.

Tumble half the rigatoni and sauce into a large (about 40 cm x 30 cm) baking dish, top with dollops of bechamel and then the remaining rigatoni and sauce. Spoon over the rest of the bechamel and sprinkle with the grated parmigiano or pecorino. Bake for 20–25 minutes until golden and bubbling, then place the mozzarella on top and bake for another 3–5 minutes or until just melted.

Finish with a sprinkle of basil leaves, if you like, and a generous grinding of pepper. Serve hot.

LASAGNE all'Abruzzese

This stunning dish is a true labour of love and one that Abruzzesi folk reserve for special occasions only, such as Christmas or Ferragosto, the Italian mid-summer feast. This traditional bake is made with silky crespelle (crepes) rather than pasta sheets, sandwiched between a rich ragù and milky mozzarella. So if you don't have a pasta machine, or simply don't feel confident making pasta from scratch, this recipe has your name all over it.

You can start this dish ahead of time if you like. Both the ragù and the crepes will keep in the fridge for 2 days. Just pile the crepes on top of each other and wrap them well.

1 quantity Ragù Abruzzese
   (see page 96)
2 eggs
80 ml (⅓ cup) milk
salt flakes and freshly ground
   black pepper
3 fresh mozzarella balls,
   thinly sliced
100 g (1 cup) freshly grated
   parmigiano

CREPES
250 g (1⅔ cups) plain flour
550 ml milk
3 eggs
40 g unsalted butter, melted
   and cooled, plus extra for
   pan-frying
salt flakes and freshly ground
   black pepper

SERVES 6–8

Make the ragù as instructed.

To prepare the crepe batter, place all the ingredients in a blender and whiz until smooth. Rest for 30 minutes.

Heat a 20 cm non-stick frying pan over medium–high heat and lightly brush with extra melted butter. Add half a ladleful of the batter and swirl to thinly coat the base, then cook for 1 minute or until the underside is light golden. Flip and cook for a further 45 seconds or until golden and cooked through. Transfer to a plate. Repeat with the remaining batter, brushing the pan with more butter as you go.

Preheat your oven to 180°C and grease a deep 20 cm round baking dish or tin.

Whisk the eggs and milk in a shallow bowl, and season well with salt and pepper.

To assemble, dip both sides of a crepe in the egg mixture, allowing any excess to drip off, then place in the dish or tin to line the base. Spoon about 3–4 tablespoons of the ragù over the top, spreading it out evenly. Top with some mozzarella slices and grated parmigiano. Repeat the layers with the remaining ingredients, finishing with mozzarella, parmigiano and any remaining egg mixture.

Cover with foil and bake for 35 minutes, then uncover and bake for a further 20 minutes or until golden and bubbling. Top with some freshly ground black pepper and serve.

RICOTTA AND spinach CANNELLONI

The beauty of cannelloni lies in their versatile nature. They can be filled with a rich meat ragù or a wonderfully nutritious vegetarian alternative. In my experience Italians are pretty evenly divided into these two camps, but speaking for myself, if ricotta and spinach is ever on offer it will always trump any carnivorous option.

100 g (1 cup) freshly grated parmigiano or pecorino
150 g (1 cup) shredded mozzarella or torn bocconcini
extra-virgin olive oil, for drizzling

FILLING
1 tablespoon extra-virgin olive oil
1 garlic clove, bashed with the back of a knife
300 g baby spinach
400 g fresh ricotta
2 eggs
75 g (¾ cup) freshly grated pecorino or parmigiano
½ teaspoon freshly grated nutmeg
finely grated zest of 1 lemon
3 tablespoons chopped flat-leaf parsley leaves
salt flakes and freshly ground black pepper

SAUCE
3 tablespoons extra-virgin olive oil
1 onion, chopped
600 ml Quick and Easy Passata (see page 29)
200 ml hot water
salt flakes
handful of basil leaves, plus extra to serve

PASTA DOUGH
300 g (2 cups) plain flour
3 eggs
salt flakes
coarse semolina, for dusting

SERVES 4–6

To make the filling, heat the olive oil in a large saucepan over medium heat. Add the garlic and spinach, then cover and cook until just wilted. Transfer to a bowl and set aside to cool. Discard the garlic, then mix through the remaining ingredients. Place in the fridge for 30 minutes.

To make the sauce, heat the olive oil in a saucepan over medium heat, add the onion and cook until soft and translucent. Add the passata and water and bring to a simmer, then reduce the heat to low and cook gently for 15 minutes. Season with salt and stir through the basil leaves.

To make the pasta dough, place the flour in a bowl, make a well in the centre and drop in the eggs and a pinch of salt. Combine using your fingers or a fork, then knead for 3–4 minutes to release the gluten and bring it together in a smooth ball. Add up to 1 tablespoon of water if it seems a bit dry. Wrap it (I use beeswax wraps) and let it rest in the fridge for 30 minutes.

Dust your board with flour or coarse semolina, and cut the dough into quarters. Work with one piece at a time and keep the rest wrapped up to prevent the dough from drying out. Flatten the dough with the palm of your hand, then pass it through the pasta machine's widest setting three or four times, folding the dough into three each time. Continue passing the dough through the machine (no further folding required) each time through a thinner setting, until you get to the second-last setting or the sheet is roughly 2.5 mm thick. Cut the pasta into 15 cm x 10 cm rectangles and dust them with semolina. Get your filling and sauce ready to start assembling the dish (you don't want to leave the sheets of pasta too long, otherwise they will dry out).

Preheat the oven to 200°C.

To assemble, smear a few tablespoons of the sauce over the base of a 40 cm x 30 cm baking dish to create a cosy bed for the cannelloni. Spoon 2–3 tablespoons of filling onto each pasta rectangle and roll up to enclose, then place, seam-side down, in the dish. Spoon the rest of the sauce over the cannelloni so that each roll is positively drowning in it. (You can add a little water to the sauce if you don't have enough.) Sprinkle the cheeses over the top and finish with a drizzle of olive oil.

Bake for 30 minutes or until nicely browned on top. Cover with foil and rest at room temperature for 20 minutes, then scatter over a few extra basil leaves and serve.

ZITI
timballo

This impressive pasta bake has graced our family table many times over the years, and there are a few tricks I have learned from Mamma along the way. Make sure you boil the pasta just until it's three-quarters cooked, then drain and rinse in cold water to arrest the cooking, otherwise the residual heat will result in overcooked pasta. It will finish cooking in the oven to al dente perfection. (Yes, I know I said earlier that you should never drain pasta, but rules are meant to be broken sometimes!)

Another trick is to reserve some of the sauce for serving. As the timballo bakes, the sauce dries out a bit and having a little extra to drizzle over the cut slices is a nice touch. Feel free to adjust the quantities to feed a larger crowd, and nothing will go wrong if you use a 20 cm springform cake tin instead of a loaf tin. You can add a little bechamel (see page 68) to the mix if you like. My mamma doesn't, but she's not going to be in your kitchen when you are creating this centrepiece, is she?

3 tablespoons extra-virgin olive oil
1 onion, chopped
1 carrot, chopped
1 celery stalk, chopped
2 garlic cloves, crushed
2 teaspoons fennel seeds, toasted and crushed
750 g pork and veal mince
3 x 400 g cans chopped tomatoes
400 g dried ziti pasta
50 g (½ cup) freshly grated parmigiano, plus extra to serve
150 g frozen peas
3–4 tablespoons dried breadcrumbs
basil leaves, to serve (optional)

SERVES 4

Heat the olive oil in a large heavy-based saucepan over medium heat. Add the onion, carrot and celery and cook for 3–4 minutes until softened, then add the garlic and fennel seeds and cook for a further 1 minute until fragrant.

Add the mince and cook, breaking up any lumps with a wooden spoon, for 8–10 minutes until well browned. Add the tomatoes and 250 ml (1 cup) of water and stir to combine, then cook for 45 minutes or until the liquid has reduced. Reserve 250 ml (1 cup) of the sauce and set aside to cool.

Preheat your oven to 180°C.

Bring a saucepan of salted water to the boil over high heat, add the ziti and cook for 5–6 minutes. You want to stop before it is al dente. Drain and rinse, then leave to cool. Set aside one-third of the ziti and cut the rest into thirds.

Combine the cut ziti, cooled mince mixture, parmigiano and peas in a bowl. Grease a 30 cm x 10 cm loaf tin with olive oil, then coat with the breadcrumbs. Line the intact ziti around the base and sides of the tin, then fill with the remaining pasta and mince mixture, compressing it down as much as possible.

Cover with foil and bake for 30 minutes. Remove from the oven and allow to cool for 15 minutes. Carefully remove the timballo from the tin and serve with extra parmigiano, basil leaves (if desired) and the reserved sauce.

PASTA
Salads

The thing about rules is there's always going to be an exception. Remember a few pages back when I was saying you should never drain or rinse your cooked pasta? Or that you should eat pasta while it's hot? Let me introduce you to the exception: pasta salad or, as we say in Italy, pasta fredda (cold). Italians turn to this versatile dish during the warmer months. It's incredibly convenient as it is eaten cold or at room temperature, which means that it can be made ahead, and it is the ideal addition to a picnic, grigliata (Italian barbecue) or summer spread. Leftovers keep well in the fridge and are wonderful in lunchboxes.

Rinsing the cooked pasta under cold water is a little trick to ensure that it stays al dente, as rinsing eliminates any residual heat that would continue to cook the pasta. It is important to note that pasta salads are only ever made with dried pasta and only a few select shapes make the cut. Farfalle, fusilli and rotelle tend to be the most popular, however penne, orecchiette and rigatoni also work well. Long strands of pasta like spaghetti or linguine will stick together like glue once cooled and become unpalatable.

PANTRY
pasta
salad

Pasta salad is always a favourite at my house during the warmer months because it allows me to clear all the leftover pasta out of my pantry.

Using 'pasta mista' (mixed pasta) in this kind of preparation is a classic and very thrifty way to make the most out of ingredients. When I do this, I look for dried pasta shapes that have similar cooking times, such as penne, rigatoni or fusilli. If your pasta bits and pieces have different cooking times, just stagger their entry into the pan so they are all ready at the same time. (I use the same idea in my minestra di pasta mista with potatoes and chickpeas on page 226.)

The pasta is then dressed with a tasty concoction of simple pantry staples, such as jarred artichokes, semi-dried tomatoes, olives, tuna and nuts – anything with an antipasto vibe! It's the ultimate pantry spring clean, with a delicious reward at the end.

400 g jar artichokes in olive oil
salt flakes
350–400 g mixed dried pasta
(such as fusilli, rigatoni, penne
or farfalle)
30 g pine nuts
280 g canned tuna in brine,
well drained
3 tablespoons olives, pitted
3 tablespoons semi-dried
tomatoes, thinly sliced
baby basil leaves, to serve

SERVES 4

Bring a large saucepan of salted water to the boil.

Meanwhile, place half the artichokes and their oil in a food processor, add a little pinch of salt and whiz until smooth. Set the dressing aside.

Cut the remaining artichokes into quarters. Heat a non-stick frying pan over medium heat, add the artichoke and fry in its oil for 2–3 minutes until slightly crisp. Set aside.

Drop the pasta into the boiling water (in batches if you need to stagger them for cooking time) and stir well, then cook until nicely al dente.

Toast the pine nuts in a hot dry frying pan until golden. This will take less than a minute, so watch them closely as they can burn easily!

Drain and rinse the pasta, reserving 125 ml (½ cup) of the pasta cooking water. Toss the pasta with the artichoke dressing, adding a little pasta cooking water if it's a bit dry. Tumble onto a platter and scatter chunks of tuna on top, followed by the olives, semi-dried tomato, pan-fried artichoke, pine nuts and baby basil leaves. So good.

Farfalle
WITH BEANS
AND zucchini
in a WALNUT
SAUCE

Do you have a vegan friend coming over for lunch? Look no further! This pasta dish is the epitome of Italian home cooking and also happens to be vegan. It's the perfect balance of protein, fibre, vitamins and carbohydrates, all bound up in a delicious, highly nutritious meal. A generous topping of lemon zest and freshly ground black pepper adds a big hit of flavour without the need for meat or dairy.

3 baby zucchini with their
   flowers
100 ml extra-virgin olive oil,
   plus extra to serve
1 zucchini, cut into 2–3 pieces
350–400 g dried farfalle pasta
   (or other short pasta)
100 g (1 cup) walnuts
¼ garlic clove
2 large handfuls of basil leaves,
   plus extra to serve
handful of mint leaves, plus
   extra to serve
salt flakes and freshly ground
   black pepper
400 g can cannellini beans,
   drained and rinsed
finely grated lemon zest,
   to serve

SERVES 4

Separate the baby zucchini from their flowers. Remove the stamen from within the petals and open the flowers up slightly. Slice the baby zucchini into thin rounds.

Heat 2 tablespoons of the olive oil in a non-stick frying pan over medium heat. Add the zucchini rounds and cook for 3–5 minutes or until golden. Set aside.

Meanwhile, bring a large saucepan of salted water to the boil. Boil the chopped zucchini for 2 minutes, then remove with a slotted spoon. Drop the pasta into the water and stir well, then cook until nicely al dente.

While the pasta is cooking, place the boiled zucchini, walnuts, garlic, herbs and remaining olive oil in a food processor and blitz until smooth. Taste for salt and adjust accordingly. Scoop into a large bowl and stir through the cannellini beans.

Drain the pasta, reserving a few tablespoons of the pasta water, and rinse it under cold water to stop the cooking. Add the pasta to the sauce, along with the cannellini beans and baby zucchini rounds, and toss to combine. Add the reserved pasta cooking water if it's a bit dry. Sprinkle over the lemon zest and top with a few extra mint and basil leaves and the zucchini flowers. Finish with a good grinding of pepper and a drizzle of extra olive oil and serve.

ROTELLE with asparagus, ricotta AND soft-boiled EGG

The wonderful combination of egg and asparagus gets upgraded to heavenly when you add al dente pasta coated in a ricotta, herb and nut dressing. The soft-boiled eggs are placed on top of the salad, and as they are opened their orange interior will gently spill out into the pasta, creating a rich, delightful sauce. If you can't find rotelle pasta, fusilli will work well, too.

4 eggs
350–400 g dried rotelle pasta
2 bunches of baby asparagus
finely grated zest of 1 lemon
50 g pecorino, shaved with
  a vegetable peeler
mint and flat-leaf parsley leaves,
  to serve
salt flakes and freshly ground
  black pepper

RICOTTA DRESSING
30 g almonds
3 tablespoons pumpkin seeds
a few large handfuls of herbs
  (mint, flat-leaf parsley and basil)
large handful of baby rocket
3 tablespoons freshly grated
  parmigiano
150 g fresh ricotta
2½ tablespoons extra-virgin
  olive oil
salt flakes and freshly ground
  black pepper

SERVES 4

Bring a small saucepan of water to the boil, gently spoon in the eggs and cook over medium heat for 6 minutes. Rinse under cold water and cool slightly, then peel and set aside.

To make the ricotta dressing, blitz the almonds and pumpkin seeds in a blender or food processor until finely ground. Add the remaining ingredients and process to form a thick dressing.

Bring a large saucepan of salted water to the boil, add the pasta and stir well, then cook until nicely al dente. Add the asparagus for the last 2 minutes of cooking.

Drain and refresh the pasta and asparagus under cold running water, then place in a large serving bowl. Add the dressing and mix to coat and combine. Top with the lemon zest, shaved pecorino, fresh herbs and halved eggs. Season with salt and pepper and serve.

Conquering GNOCCHI

These delicious dumplings definitely need their own chapter. Whether they are made with potatoes, ricotta, pumpkin, stale bread (see page 236) or semolina, gnocchi are always a festive dish at every Italian table.

Back in post-war Italy, gnocchi used to be a weekly occurrence, made every Giovedí (Thursday). 'Giovedí Gnocchi' was not simply a folkloristic habit – the satiating nature of a large bowl (or two) of gnocchi for Thursday supper meant that the religious requirement of only consuming light meals on Friday could be endured more easily. And although religious calendars are not observed so strictly these days, the saying has stuck, and in most trattorias, especially around Rome, you will find that the dish of the day on Thursdays is indeed gnocchi.

But why is it that something so little and humble can inspire such dread in home cooks?

Many people have confessed to me their anxieties over these Italian dumplings, whether they become hard and knobbly, or turn into one massive lump once cooked, or literally disintegrate into the boiling water. We can all understand the frustration of labouring in the kitchen only to see it all turn to goo!

Hopefully after delving into this chapter you will no longer fear making gnocchi from scratch! And for my tips to help you avoid kitchen disasters and guarantee perfect gnocchi every time, please turn the page.

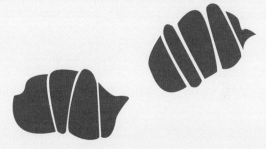

Conquering GNOCCHI

Tips for Making Perfect Gnocchi

1. **NOT ALL POTATOES ARE BORN EQUAL!** The best potatoes to use for gnocchi are floury ones with a low water content, such as desiree or russet (the ones with red skin). Slightly older potatoes are even better, as they retain less moisture.

2. **BOIL THEM WHOLE!** Think of the skin as a protective barrier that stops water from penetrating your tubers. My mamma's trick is to fit them very snugly in a pan so they can barely move; she then fills the pan with cold water and adds two fistfuls of salt. I know this seems excessive, but the salty water will protect the skin from cracking, preventing the potatoes from absorbing extra water. And the added bonus is that the cooked potatoes are perfectly seasoned.

Some people suggest baking the potatoes on a bed of salt, which is also a clever way to keep them dry. Your choice. If you are making pumpkin gnocchi, roasting the pumpkin first will help the moisture to evaporate.

4. **DON'T ADD TOO MUCH FLOUR.** The first time you make gnocchi it may seem that the dough is too soft and you'll be tempted to add more flour. I urge you to resist. The more flour you add, the tougher your gnocchi will be.

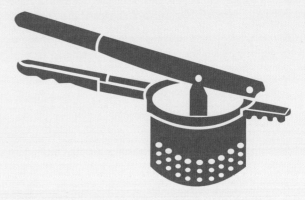

5. **INVEST IN A POTATO RICER.** Of course you can use a masher (I've even used a fork a few times) and if you don't mind a few lumps, go right ahead. But if you're after a smoother texture, a potato ricer will be your new best friend.

"Nyoh-kee"

3. **PEEL THEM WHILE THEY ARE STILL HOT.** Yes, I realise hot potatoes are hard to handle, but if you leave it until they have cooled the skin will start to stick to the cooked potato. I don't mean boiling hot – by all means let them cool for 10 minutes, but that's about it. Use gloves if need be. After a while you'll probably find your tolerance to heat will increase. Asbestos hands!

6. **DON'T OVERCOOK THEM!** Gnocchi tell you when they are ready so watch them closely and get them out of the boiling water as soon as they float to the surface. Overcooked gnocchi will quickly start to disintegrate into the boiling water.

One other thing that can break the heart of an Italian is when the word 'gnocchi' is mispronounced ... the first letter is silent. In Italy we proudly pronounce them 'nyoh-kee', and you really want to hit that K sound with a passion!

BASIC potato gnocchi

If you took a moment to read my gnocchi tips opposite, you will know that making a successful gnocchi dough is all about knowing the type of potatoes to use and how to cook and handle them. It really is easy – just be confident!

850 g starchy potatoes (russet or desiree), unpeeled
salt flakes
1 egg yolk
110–150 g (¾–1 cup) plain or type '00' flour

SERVES 4

Place the whole potatoes snugly in a large saucepan. Fill with cold water, add two fistfuls of salt and bring to the boil over high heat. Cook for 35–40 minutes or until tender. Drain well, then set aside for 10 minutes until cool enough to handle.

Pass the potatoes through a potato ricer and allow to cool for about 5–10 minutes. Stir in the egg yolk and a small pinch of salt. (If you don't have a ricer, you can use a masher instead, although you will need to peel the potatoes first.)

Start adding the flour, a little at a time. Depending on your potatoes and the type of flour you use, you may need to use a little more or less than indicated. You want a soft dough that is pliable and not tacky. I normally end up using about three-quarters and use the rest for dusting while I'm shaping the gnocchi. Don't be tempted to add too much flour or your gnocchi will be heavy.

Cut the dough into four or five pieces, then place on a floured surface and roll them into 2 cm thick logs. Cut each log into 2–3 cm pieces.

You can leave them like that if you like. Alternatively, roll them over a wooden gnocchi board or press them against the tines of a fork to form ridges – gently but like you mean it. The tines will leave indentations in the gnocchi, ready to trap the sauce for the joy of your palate.

Once you have rolled all your gnocchi, dust them with flour and set aside. They are best cooked within a few hours.

Baked POTATO GNOCCHI alla Sorrentina

If you've always thought a steaming bowl of gnocchi is the epitome of comfort food, picture a baking dish full of these nuggets, coated in luscious red sugo and dotted with stretchy mozzarella. This is the way they do it in Sorrento, and it is as magnificent as it sounds.

1 quantity Basic Potato Gnocchi (see page 91)
1 quantity Sugo (see page 28)
220 g tub bocconcini, drained
3 tablespoons freshly grated parmigiano
freshly ground black pepper
basil leaves, to serve

SERVES 4

Make the gnocchi and sugo as instructed.

Preheat your oven to 180°C.

Bring a large saucepan of salted water to the boil and cook your gnocchi in batches. As soon as they float to the surface fish them out with a slotted spoon and drop them straight into the sugo. Toss to coat and encourage the flavours to mingle.

Transfer the gnocchi and sugo to a baking dish. Top with the bocconcini and parmigiano and bake for 15–20 minutes or until the cheese has melted and the sauce is bubbling. Finish with a grinding of pepper and a few basil leaves and serve.

Potato GNOCCHI all'Abruzzese with ragù

The Abruzzese home cook is never fussed about looks as flavour is what matters most, so local food preparation tends to err on the 'rustic' side, well compensated for with generous portions and robust piquancy. Gone are the pretty ridges, Abruzzese cooks simply cut the logs of dough into diamonds. Gnocchi are often served with lamb ragù (see page 24), sugo (see page 28) or this Abruzzese-style ragù, which is flavoured with pancetta and juniper berries and is typical of the area.

1 quantity Basic Potato Gnocchi
    dough (see page 91)
freshly grated pecorino, to serve
freshly ground white pepper,
    to serve

RAGÙ ABRUZZESE

3 tablespoons extra-virgin
    olive oil
50 g piece of pancetta or speck
1 carrot, chopped
1 onion, chopped
1 celery stalk, chopped
1 garlic clove, skin on, bashed
    with the back of a knife
5–6 juniper berries, crushed
500 g pork and beef mince
200 ml red wine
3 x 400 g cans chopped
    tomatoes
2 teaspoons tomato paste
500 ml (2 cups) good-quality
    beef or chicken stock
1–2 bay leaves
salt flakes and freshly ground
    white pepper

SERVES 4

To make the ragù Abruzzese, heat the olive oil in a heavy-based saucepan over medium–low heat. Add the pancetta or speck and cook gently for 2–3 minutes, then add the carrot, onion, celery, garlic and juniper berries and cook over medium heat until the onion is soft and translucent. Drop in the pork and beef mince and brown over high heat for 5 minutes, breaking up any lumps with a wooden spoon.

Deglaze the pan with the wine, scraping up any bits caught on the base, and simmer until the alcohol has evaporated (this should take about 2 minutes). Add the tomatoes, tomato paste and stock and bring to a simmer, then reduce the heat to low. Add the bay leaves and season with salt, then cover and cook slowly for 3–4 hours, stirring occasionally. Add a little water if it starts to dry out, but keep in mind that the sauce needs to reduce and thicken.

Taste for salt and adjust accordingly, and season with white pepper. You probably won't need all the ragù for the gnocchi – start with half, and if you think you need more, add it later. Store the leftovers in an airtight container in the freezer for up to 6 months.

While the ragù is simmering away, make the gnocchi dough as instructed. To shape them, roll the dough into logs as you would for classic gnocchi, then cut the logs diagonally into diamond shapes, roughly 2.5 cm long.

Make a bed of ragù on a large serving platter.

Bring a large saucepan of salted water to the boil and cook your gnocchi in batches. As soon as they float to the surface fish them out with a slotted spoon and drop them straight onto the platter, tossing them gently in the ragù. Add a bit more ragù as you add more gnocchi, then toss to coat and encourage the flavours to mingle.

Sprinkle with freshly grated pecorino and white pepper and serve hot.

Basic PUMPKIN gnocchi

One of the many virtues of gnocchi is its versatility: you can swap its main ingredient and still create a sensational dish. While potato gnocchi are more mainstream, pumpkin gnocchi have quietly developed a following too, and because they offer a vibrant colour and delectable sweetness they carry a little more of a 'wow' factor. Very much like potato gnocchi, they are easy to make – just be sure to select the right type of pumpkin and roast it first to remove excess moisture.

900 g peeled and deseeded kent pumpkin, cut into small chunks
2 tablespoons extra-virgin olive oil
salt flakes and freshly ground white pepper
1 egg yolk
220–270 g plain or type '00' flour, plus extra for dusting

SERVES 4

Preheat your oven to 200°C and line a baking tray with baking paper.

Place the pumpkin on the prepared tray, drizzle with the olive oil and season with salt and white pepper. Roast for 40–45 minutes or until tender, then transfer to a large bowl and mash until smooth. Set aside to cool for 15 minutes, then mix in the egg yolk and season again.

Add 220 g of the flour and mix through. Check the consistency – if it's too tacky, gradually add the rest of the flour, stopping as soon as the dough is soft and smooth. The water content in pumpkins can vary and this affects the quantity of flour needed, so take this step slowly.

Cut the dough into six or eight pieces, roll them into 2 cm thick logs and cut each log into 2 cm pieces. (You will find that pumpkin gnocchi are a little more delicate than those made with potato so I wouldn't roll them on a gnocchi board to create ridges as they may stick.) Dust your gnocchi with flour and set aside. They are best cooked within a few hours.

PUMPKIN gnocchi WITH honey burnt butter, SAGE and WALNUTS

Burnt butter sauces are a wondrous culinary hack. There is no real recipe involved – you simply watch your butter like a hawk as it quickly turns from pale yellow to deep gold. Add a touch of honey and you have the makings of a stunning dish. Just toss with cooked gnocchi, dust with as much cheese as you like and sprinkle with crunchy walnuts.

1 quantity Basic Pumpkin
  Gnocchi (see page 99)
75 g unsalted butter
1 tablespoon extra-virgin olive oil
10–12 sage leaves, or to taste
1 tablespoon honey
50 g (½ cup) walnuts, roughly
  chopped
salt flakes and freshly ground
  black pepper
freshly grated parmigiano,
  to serve

SERVES 4

Make the gnocchi dough as instructed.

Bring a large saucepan of salted water to the boil.

Meanwhile, combine the butter, olive oil and sage leaves in a large saucepan over medium heat and cook until the butter has melted and turned a light nut brown. Stir through the honey.

Toss the walnuts into a small frying pan over medium heat and toast for 30–45 seconds or until you can smell their aroma. Watch carefully as they burn very easily!

Working in batches, cook your gnocchi in the boiling water. As soon as they float to the surface fish them out with a slotted spoon and drop them straight in the butter sauce, tossing gently to coat. The starchy cooking water you are dragging along (acqua di cottura) will help create a luscious sauce. Season to taste with salt and pepper.

Take the pan off the heat, add a good sprinkling of parmigiano and stir until melted and combined. Season with salt and pepper, top with the toasted walnuts and serve.

Pumpkin GNOCCHI with MUSSELS AND borlotti

When cooking mussels always make sure the shells are scrubbed to remove any barnacles and debris. These days mussels are often sold pre-cleaned and all that's left to do is remove the beard – that clump of hair-like fibres that sprouts from the shell. To do this, grab the beard with your thumb and forefinger and tug it towards the hinge of the shell. Discard any mussels with broken shells, or open shells that don't close when you tap them. Basically, you don't want anything interfering with the integrity of the mollusc within.

For this recipe I tend to use canned borlotti beans, but if you can get your hands on fresh ones they are truly amazing. You just need to cook them in unsalted boiling water for 45 minutes. If you would like to use dried beans, soak them overnight, then boil in unsalted water for 1–1½ hours until tender. Allow to cool in the cooking water and only season after they are cooked or they will wrinkle up!

1 quantity Basic Pumpkin Gnocchi (see page 99)
400 g mussels, cleaned and debearded
150 ml dry white wine
3 tablespoons extra-virgin olive oil
1 spring onion, white and green parts finely chopped
1 garlic clove, finely chopped
200 g canned borlotti beans, drained and rinsed
salt flakes and freshly ground black pepper
finely chopped flat-leaf parsley leaves, to serve

SERVES 4

Make the gnocchi dough as instructed.

Bring a large saucepan of salted water to the boil.

Meanwhile, place a large heavy-based saucepan over medium–high heat and add the mussels and wine. Cover with a lid and allow the steam to open the shells (this will take 2–3 minutes). As they open, lift them out with a slotted spoon and set aside. Pass the cooking liquid through a strainer and reserve for later.

Wipe the pan clean with paper towel, then add the olive oil, spring onion and garlic and cook over medium heat for 1 minute or until fragrant (watch it closely as garlic can burn quickly). Add the beans and reserved mussel cooking liquid and cook for 1–2 minutes.

Working in batches, cook your gnocchi in the boiling water. As soon as they float to the surface fish them out with a slotted spoon and drop them straight into the bean mixture.

Toss well over medium heat to allow the starches from the gnocchi to bind the sauce together and thicken it. Season to taste with salt and pepper.

Remove the pan from the heat and add the mussels. Finish with a little chopped parsley and serve hot.

Basic RICOTTA GNOCCHI

If you are still feeling a little sceptical about potato gnocchi, you'll be happy to know Italy is also known for its light pillows of ricotta gnocchi. The dough comes together in 3 minutes flat and, because of their high protein content, ricotta gnocchi offer more in terms of nutrition, too. Win–win!

450 g fresh ricotta
2 egg yolks
½ teaspoon salt flakes
3 tablespoons finely chopped flat-leaf parsley, basil and chives
100–120 g plain or type '00' flour, plus extra for dusting
50 g (½ cup) freshly grated parmigiano
extra-virgin olive oil, for drizzling

SERVES 4

Discard any excess liquid from the ricotta, then put it in a large mixing bowl with the egg yolks, salt and herbs. Add 100 g (⅔ cup) of the flour and the parmigiano and work with floured hands or a wooden spoon until you have a smooth, soft dough – gradually add the remaining flour if it seems a little tacky. It should be pliable and a little sticky but not too wet. Don't be tempted to add lots of flour to make it easier to work the dough as the resulting gnocchi will almost certainly be dense and doughy.

Flour your hands and cooking bench generously and cut the dough into six pieces. Working with one piece at a time, sprinkle it with flour and roll it with your hands to form a 2 cm thick log. Cut the log into 1 cm pieces and set them aside on a floured wooden board. Repeat with the remaining dough. Set aside.

Ricotta gnocchi with pancetta, PEAS AND broad beans

Around March in Italy, an abundance of green pods adorning market baskets heralds the beginning of spring. Italian home cooks know their season is too short to be caught unawares and we buy them by the bucketload. I have to admit most of the broad beans I pod immediately find their way into my belly, their natural flavour untouched by a single extraneous ingredient, but they are equally divine cooked. Here's my offering: a simple combination of sweet peas, salty pancetta and nutty broad beans paired with fluffy ricotta gnocchi.

1 quantity Basic Ricotta Gnocchi
   (see opposite)
3 tablespoons extra-virgin
   olive oil
2 golden shallots, thinly sliced
4 thin slices of pancetta, cut
   into strips
1 garlic clove, skin on, bashed
   with the back of a knife
salt flakes and freshly ground
   black pepper
200 g podded and peeled
   broad beans
155 g (1 cup) freshly shelled
   (or frozen) peas

TO SERVE
finely grated lemon zest
mint leaves
freshly grated pecorino

SERVES 4

Make the gnocchi dough as instructed.

Bring a large saucepan of salted water to the boil.

Heat the olive oil in a large heavy-based frying pan over medium heat, add the shallot, pancetta, garlic and a pinch of salt and saute for 2–3 minutes until the shallot is softened and the pancetta is crispy. Add the broad beans and peas and cook, tossing, for 1–2 minutes. Remove from the heat and season with salt and pepper.

Working in batches, cook your gnocchi in the boiling water. As soon as they float to the surface fish them out with a slotted spoon and drop them straight into the broad bean mixture. Toss over medium heat to encourage the flavours to mingle. Add a little cooking water if it seems a bit dry. Sprinkle with lemon zest, mint leaves and pecorino and serve.

Ricotta GNOCCHI with quick prawn RAGÙ

Here's a dish that looks so impressive people will assume you have been labouring in the kitchen for hours. In fact, it comes together in less than half an hour, including making the gnocchi from scratch. Don't tell your friends though ... this beauty will earn you masses of brownie points!

Something rather exciting happens when you treat prawn meat like mince. The edges turn crispy and caramelised, attracting all the sugars from the tomatoes and wine to cling to its unruly surface. Such a pleasure to see, but more importantly to eat.

1 quantity Basic Ricotta Gnocchi (see page 104)
2 tablespoons extra-virgin olive oil
1 spring onion, white and green parts finely chopped
1 long red chilli, thinly sliced
1 tablespoon finely chopped flat-leaf parsley stalks
1 garlic clove, thinly sliced
10 prawns, peeled, deveined and roughly chopped
400 g cherry tomatoes, halved
125 ml (½ cup) dry white wine
salt flakes
chopped flat-leaf parsley leaves, to serve

SERVES 4

Make the gnocchi dough as instructed.

Bring a large saucepan of salted water to the boil.

Meanwhile, heat the olive oil in a large saucepan over medium heat, add the spring onion, chilli and parsley stalks and cook for 1 minute. Add the garlic and prawn meat and cook, stirring, for 1 minute. Toss in the cherry tomatoes, then deglaze the pan with the wine, scraping up any bits caught on the base, and cook for 2 minutes or until the alcohol has evaporated. Remove from the heat.

Working in batches, cook your gnocchi in the boiling water. As soon as they float to the surface fish them out with a slotted spoon and drop them straight into the sauce.

Toss well to encourage the flavours to mingle, and season to taste with some salt. Sprinkle with chopped parsley and serve immediately.

Semolina GNOCCHI ALLA Romana

Quite different from traditional potato or ricotta gnocchi, gnocchi alla Romana (Roman style) are made with semolina flour and cooked more like polenta than classic gnocchi. The cooked semolina is cooled and cut into rounds, then layered into a dish and baked until slightly crispy on the outside and soft and custard-like on the inside. It truly is the stuff of dreams.

750 ml (3 cups) milk
¼ teaspoon freshly grated nutmeg
75 g unsalted butter, chopped
225 g semolina flour (see note page 38)
salt flakes and freshly ground black pepper
2 egg yolks
75 g (¾ cup) freshly grated parmigiano
40 g freshly grated pecorino

SERVES 4–6

Line a baking tray with baking paper and grease a 30 cm x 20 cm baking dish with olive oil.

Pour the milk into a medium saucepan, add the nutmeg and 30 g of the butter and bring to a simmer over medium heat. Add the semolina flour and whisk vigorously for 8–10 minutes or until thick and lump free. Season with salt and pepper. Add the egg yolks and parmigiano and mix through until melted and smooth.

Turn out onto the lined baking tray and pat the mixture out evenly to a 2 cm thickness. Set aside to cool completely. As it cools down it will set firm.

Preheat your oven to 200°C.

Cut the cooled mixture into 4–5 cm rounds using an oiled cookie cutter or tumbler. Overlap the rounds in the greased baking dish, top with the pecorino and dot with the remaining butter. Bake for 20–25 minutes or until bubbly and the edges are golden brown.

The TRUTH about RICE AND risotto

Not all rice dishes in Italy are risotto. In fact, the term 'risotto' refers to a particular cooking technique that is mainly applied to short-grain rice, but can also be used to cook cereal grains, such as barley or even pasta (see page 59). In this chapter I will help you navigate the world of Italian rice dishes, from Venetian risi e bisi and risotto Milanese right down to Sicilian arancini.

There are three main types of rice used in Italian cooking: arborio, carnaroli and vialone nano. Arborio and carnaroli are high-starch short-grain varieties and are best suited for risotto making. Vialone nano can also be used in risotto, but its higher starch content also makes it perfect for soup preparations, like minestrone or risi e bisi.

Now that we are clear on rice grains it's time to address the elephant in the room … risotto can make people incredibly anxious, especially, it seems, if you are under pressure on reality TV! How many aspiring chefs have tried and failed to beat the curse of the gluggy risotto?

Very much like pasta and gnocchi making, there are some fundamental dos and don'ts that can make or break your risotto and, by extension, your self-esteem. I have laid out my ten rules for creating perfect risotto over the page.

PS Please, please, under no circumstances add poultry, beef, haloumi, pesto or feta to risotto! And if you must, don't tell any Italians …

And one final point: if prepared in a slow cooker or other extravagant kitchen gadget, it's not risotto – it's just a yummy rice dish.

The TRUTH about Rice and RISOTTO

My 10 Rules for Perfect Risotto

1. NOT ALL RICE GRAINS ARE SUITED FOR RISOTTO. As mentioned on page 112, carnaroli and arborio are the best ones to use. Under no circumstances try it with jasmine or basmati rice!

2. USE GOOD STOCK. Your risotto is only ever going to be as good as your stock. No matter how stunning the other ingredients are, if the flavour is not established by the liquid component, your risotto will suffer. If you can use homemade, please go for it. If that is not an option, then you can spruce up bought liquid stocks, powders or cubes by adding a few fresh ingredients, such as carrot, onion (even just onion peel), parsley, chicken bones and any leftover greens you may have in the fridge. Make sure your stock is well seasoned, though taste it first as some bought stocks can be very salty.

3. TOAST YOUR RICE GRAINS WELL. It's important to toast the rice before adding the wine and the stock. This creates a barrier that will stop your rice from going mushy.

4. BE GENTLE. Once you start adding the stock, reduce the heat to medium–low. Risotto appreciates a bit of gentle heat.

5. DON'T OVER-STIR! I cannot stress this enough. You only need a light stir to make sure each grain of rice is well covered in stock after each addition. Constant vigorous stirring throughout the cooking time will release too much starch too soon, resulting in a gluey mess.

6. USE THE RIGHT PAN. Don't use a stockpot or large saucepan for risotto making. Rice grains do better in a heavy-based frying pan with a side about 10 cm high. I always use a non-stick one, as it makes cleaning that much easier.

7. DON'T OVERCOOK YOUR RICE. This little-known truth about risotto may shock some, but in Italy we enjoy it al dente. Very much like when you are cooking dried pasta (see page 51), if the packet suggests 18–20 minutes, turn the heat off after 16–17 minutes at the most. The residual heat will continue cooking it to perfection. Overcooked rice is truly unpalatable and gives your risotto the texture of baby food.

8. HONOUR THE MANTECATURA! This is the name given to the final stage of risotto making. After you turn off the heat, add butter and parmigiano and stir *like you mean it* for 30–45 seconds to release all the starches. Add one ladleful of stock, cover with a lid and leave to rest for 2 minutes, allowing the steam to finish cooking the rice grains. When you remove the lid you will see that the rice has turned into risotto, with its signature creamy, slightly wet texture we like to call 'all'onda' (like a wave).

9. DON'T LET RISOTTO SIT AROUND. It must be eaten straight after mantecatura. Serve it in shallow rather than deep bowls to avoid piling up the hot rice, which will invariably lead to overcooked mush. Leftovers can be repurposed into delicious meals, like timballo, arancini and the underrated but exquisite riso al salto (see pages 130, 135 and 132)

10. ENJOY THE PROCESS! Risotto is no big deal. It cooks faster than you think and it really only requires a little love to reach its potential, so relax and enjoy it.

CLASSIC risotto parmigiana

Once you master this, you will have the confidence to attempt more complex risotto recipes. But don't be fooled by the humble appearance of this dish — it is rich and flavourful, especially if you build on the solid foundation of a robust stock.

1 tablespoon extra-virgin olive oil
50 g butter
1 white onion, diced
350 g carnaroli or arborio rice
200 ml dry white wine
2 litres good-quality chicken or vegetable stock, brought to a gentle simmer
50 g (½ cup) freshly grated parmigiano, plus extra to serve (optional)
salt flakes and freshly ground black or white pepper

SERVES 4

Heat the olive oil and half the butter in a large heavy-based frying pan over medium heat. Add the onion and cook until soft and translucent, but not caramelised. Add the rice and stir until well coated in the oil and butter.

Add the wine and allow the alcohol to evaporate, stirring occasionally (this will take 1–2 minutes). Reduce the heat to medium–low and start adding the stock, a couple of ladlefuls at a time, giving it the occasional gentle stir. Keep adding the stock until the rice is al dente, about 16–17 minutes.

Remove the pan from the heat and add a final ladleful of stock, the parmigiano and remaining butter. Taste for salt and adjust to your liking, then season with pepper. Stir vigorously to release the starch and create an all'onda texture. Cover with a lid and let it rest for a few minutes to create the perfect mantecatura (creaminess). Ladle into shallow bowls and serve with some extra parmigiano and black pepper, if you like.

RISOTTO ALLA Milanese
with saffron AND bone marrow

I thought long and hard about whether I should feature this recipe in this book. The Milanese born-and-bred girl in me would obviously want to, but on the other hand I know that this recipe, like many classic Italian dishes, can create controversy. I have chef friends who swear that true risotto alla Milanese should have shallot rather than onion, while others argue that onion is not needed at all. Some like to cook the marrow separately with onion and butter, then whiz it and use it as a paste to flavour the rice (nice idea!). And there are those who will only serve risotto Milanese with osso buco and gremolata, which is indeed a wondrous thing. So who's right? Is anyone actually wrong? My answer is no. I think that some differences are to be expected when making a dish that dates back to 1574 when, legend has it, it was created to celebrate a famous glass master from Milan and served at his daughter's wedding feast. Since saffron was used to tint the glass of church windows (and those of the famous Duomo cathedral) it was added to a rice dish to honour the work of the bride's father. Over the centuries the recipe was lost and then found a few times until it was finally recorded in a written collection in the early 1800s.

1 tablespoon extra-virgin olive oil
50 g butter
1 golden shallot, finely chopped
40 g bone marrow, finely chopped (see note)
350 g carnaroli or arborio rice
200 ml dry white wine
2 litres good-quality chicken or beef stock, brought to a gentle simmer
1 teaspoon saffron threads mixed with a ladleful of stock
50 g (½ cup) freshly grated parmigiano
salt flakes

SERVES 4

Heat the olive oil and half the butter in a large heavy-based frying pan over medium heat. Add the shallot and cook for 2 minutes, then add the bone marrow and cook until the shallot is soft and translucent but not caramelised, and the marrow has melted into the mixture. Add the rice and stir until well coated in the butter and bone marrow mixture.

Add the wine and allow the alcohol to evaporate, stirring occasionally (this will take 1–2 minutes). Reduce the heat to medium–low and start adding the stock, a couple of ladlefuls at a time, giving it the occasional gentle stir. Keep adding the stock until the rice is al dente, about 16–17 minutes. Halfway through cooking, add the saffron-infused stock.

Remove the pan from the heat and add a final ladleful of stock, the parmigiano and remaining butter. Taste for salt and adjust to your liking. Stir vigorously to release the starch and create an all'onda texture. Cover with a lid and let it rest for a few minutes for the perfect mantecatura (creaminess). Ladle into shallow bowls and serve.

NOTE
I get bone marrow from my local butcher, who kindly takes it out of the bones and cleans it for me. As it cooks in the onion and butter it melts, creating the richest, most luscious base for this ancient dish. If bone marrow is hard to come by, it's okay to skip it. Not all recipes for risotto Milanese feature this ingredient.

RISOTTO
with
asparagus and prawns

This elegant dish ticks all the boxes when it comes to flavour, texture and presentation. The combination of blushing pink prawns and vibrant green asparagus offers a pretty palette, with a subtle sweetness and earthy aromas. You will notice there is no parmigiano added to the mantecatura; this is because, with a few notable exceptions, Italians prefer to let the delicate flavour of seafood shine through.

1 bunch of asparagus
12 raw prawns
2 tablespoons extra-virgin olive oil
40 g butter
350 g carnaroli or arborio rice
200 ml dry white wine
2 litres good-quality vegetable stock, brought to a gentle simmer
salt flakes and freshly ground black pepper
finely grated lemon zest, to serve

SERVES 4

Trim the woody ends off the asparagus and peel the spears if they are thick. Cut the stems into 2 cm pieces, keeping the tips intact. Set aside.

Peel and devein the prawns. You can add the prawn shells and heads to your stock for extra flavour if you like.

Heat the olive oil and half the butter in a large heavy-based frying pan over medium heat. Add the rice and stir until well coated in the oil and butter.

Add the wine and allow the alcohol to evaporate, stirring occasionally (this will take 1–2 minutes). Reduce the heat to medium–low and start adding the stock, a couple of ladlefuls at a time, giving it the occasional gentle stir. Keep adding the stock until the rice is almost al dente, about 15–16 minutes.

Add the asparagus and toss through, then taste and season with salt and pepper. Remove the pan from the heat and add the remaining butter and another ladleful of stock. Stir vigorously to release the starch and create an all'onda texture. Add the prawns, then cover with a lid and let it rest for a few minutes to create the perfect mantecatura (creaminess). The residual heat will cook the prawns. Ladle into shallow bowls, sprinkle with lemon zest and black pepper and serve.

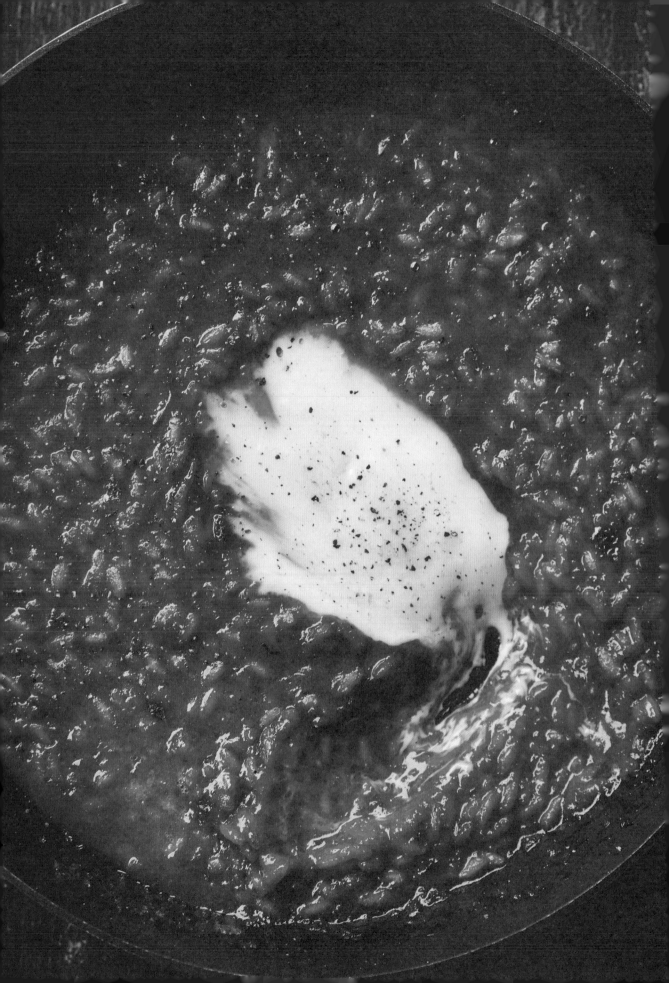

Risotto with roasted beetroot AND stracchino

As well as being stunning to the eye, this combination of creamy rice and sweet, nutty beetroot tastes sensational. You could serve it as it is – it's certainly rich enough – but do try to get your hands on some stracchino cheese from your local Italian deli. Add it while your risotto is resting and watch as the residual heat gently melts it to creamy deliciousness.

3 beetroots
salt flakes and freshly ground black pepper
3 tablespoons extra-virgin olive oil
50 g butter
1 red onion, finely chopped
350 g carnaroli or arborio rice
200 ml dry white wine
2 litres good-quality vegetable or chicken stock, brought to a gentle simmer
50 g (½ cup) freshly grated parmigiano
150 g stracchino cheese (see note)
thyme leaves, to serve (optional)

SERVES 4

Preheat your oven to 200°C.

Wrap the beetroots in foil and roast for about 1 hour or until soft. Peel off the skin and puree the flesh in a food processor, then season with a little salt and pepper. Set aside.

Heat 1 tablespoon of the olive oil and half of the butter in a large heavy-based frying pan over medium heat. Add the onion and cook until soft and translucent, but not caramelised. Add the rice and stir to coat in the oil and butter.

Add the wine and allow the alcohol to evaporate, stirring occasionally (this will take 1–2 minutes). Reduce the heat to medium–low and start adding the stock, a couple of ladlefuls at a time, giving it the occasional gentle stir. Keep adding the stock until the rice is al dente, about 16–17 minutes.

Remove the pan from the heat and add a final ladleful of stock, the beetroot puree, parmigiano and remaining butter. Taste and season with salt and pepper. Stir vigorously to release the starch and create the all'onda texture. Top with the stracchino, then cover with a lid and let it rest for a few minutes to create the perfect mantecatura (creaminess). Grind over some more black pepper, then ladle the risotto into shallow bowls. Top with a scattering of thyme leaves, if you like, and serve.

NOTE
If you can't find stracchino, stracciatella is a very good alternative.

Baked RICE-STUFFED tomatoes

This Roman classic speaks volumes about Italian home cooking: just a couple of simple ingredients that bring out the best in each other. The tomato juices, olive oil and rice bake together to create textures that are both soft and crispy, while the precious juices coat the potato wedges, which instantly steal the spotlight. (Make more than you think you'll need. I'm serious.)

You may find the quantity of rice in the recipe is slightly odd, but it reflects the Italian approach to home cooking, which generally means not measuring with scales. The idea is to fill each tomato with 2 tablespoons of rice and, to be honest, this is the most accurate an Italian nonna is ever going to be! This dish is also incredibly forgiving so if you are heavy-handed with your rice or pecorino, you're not going to upset anybody.

6–7 large truss tomatoes
salt flakes and freshly ground
    black pepper
3–4 tablespoons freshly
    grated pecorino, plus extra
    for sprinkling
thyme leaves, to taste
100 ml extra-virgin olive oil
12–14 tablespoons carnaroli or
    arborio rice
4 potatoes, peeled and each
    potato cut into eight wedges
3–4 garlic cloves, crushed
a few thyme or rosemary sprigs
chilli oil, to serve (optional)

SERVES 4–6

Preheat your oven to 200°C and line a baking tray with baking paper (or grease with olive oil).

Cut the top off each tomato and set aside. Scoop out the pulp and place in a bowl, then season the hollow tomatoes with salt. Using your hands, squeeze out as much liquid as possible from the pulp and break it down with a fork. Season the tomato pulp and juice with salt and pepper and stir in the pecorino, thyme leaves and 2 tablespoons of the olive oil. Add the rice and combine.

Spoon 2 tablespoons of the rice mixture into each tomato and place in the prepared tray. Add 1–2 tablespoons of water to each tomato to help the rice cook evenly, then put the tomato lids on top. Drizzle 2 tablespoons of the olive oil over the tomatoes and season with an extra pinch of salt.

Place the potato wedges in a bowl, add the garlic and remaining olive oil, then season with salt and pepper. Toss together, then arrange the potato in the tray around the tomatoes and top with some thyme or rosemary sprigs.

Bake for 35–40 minutes or until the tomatoes are scorched, the rice is cooked through and the potato wedges are golden. Take the lids off the tomatoes and sprinkle a little pecorino over the rice filling. Return to the oven for another 5–10 minutes to create a crust.

Take the tray out of the oven and put the tomato lids back on. You can enjoy this hot, or cover with foil and rest for 20 minutes, then serve warm with a splash of chilli oil, if you like.

RISI e BISI (Rice AND PEAS)

Just when you thought you'd cracked the art of gradually adding stock and gently stirring risotto to creamy perfection, enter a much-loved rice dish from the north of Italy that will only really work if you add most of the stock at once and don't stir it! What's all that about? I suppose you would call it 'regional diversity' and Italy – a country comprising twenty-one regions, each proudly showcasing their dialect, heritage and cuisine – is solidly built on it.

The disarming simplicity of risi e bisi (rice and peas in the vernacular from the Veneto region) encapsulates all that is great about Italian peasant cuisine. A few humble ingredients, sourced locally at the peak of their season, produce what is effectively the love child of risotto and rice soup. But if you value your life, don't ever call this dish a risotto in front of a local! They will give you a stern look and quite possibly a lecture on rice in an incomprehensible accent.

To be honest, I think any local would disapprove of my suggestion to use frozen peas, as in Veneto they only use fresh and add the empty pods to the stock for an extra pea boost. Please feel free to follow tradition if you prefer, but when life gets in the way of shelling fresh peas, try this simple recipe – it may well become a mid-week favourite for children and grown-ups alike. And if you wish to keep this strictly vegetarian, omit the pancetta.

1 tablespoon extra-virgin olive oil
40 g butter
2 golden shallots, finely chopped
30 g piece of smoked pancetta
320 g vialone nano or arborio rice
1.5 litres good-quality chicken stock, brought to a gentle simmer
235 g (1½ cups) frozen peas
35 g (⅓ cup) freshly grated parmigiano, plus extra to serve (optional)
salt flakes and freshly ground black pepper

SERVES 4

Heat the olive oil and half the butter in a large saucepan over medium heat. Add the shallot and pancetta and cook until the shallot is soft and translucent, but not caramelised. Add the rice and stir until well coated in the oil and butter.

Add three-quarters of the stock and bring to a simmer, then cook over medium–low heat for 10 minutes. Stir in the peas and cook for a further 6–7 minutes or until the rice is al dente, very gently stirring occasionally to prevent the rice from sticking.

Remove the pan from the heat. Add the remaining stock and butter and the parmigiano and stir well to release the starch. Season with salt and pepper.

Ladle into bowls and serve with some extra parmigiano, if you like.

NOTES
If it looks like the liquid is being absorbed too quickly during cooking, add a bit more water or stock.

The smoked pancetta is there to flavour the dish. I always leave it in, but you can discard it before serving if you prefer.

SARTÙ di riso (Neapolitan rice timballo)

This rice timballo has many virtues: it's gluten free (as long as you use gluten-free breadcrumbs for the tin), which is something many people will be excited about; unlike its pasta cousin, it's as good warm as it is at room temperature, making it the ideal prepare-ahead dish; and it is very substantial. Hidden within the layers of ragù-coated rice you will find eggs, cheese and salami, so a little goes a long way!

In Naples they often replace the salami with mini meatballs, which is sensationally delicious, albeit a bit more laborious. It can also be transformed into a vegetarian dish by using sugo (see page 28), provola (or even mozzarella), peas and eggs as the filling. I have even made it with just sugo and cheese as I didn't have eggs or peas on hand, and it still delivered on both flavour and looks. Don't be afraid to customise it, although I would steer clear of the 'prohibited' ingredients outlined in the chapter introduction (see page 112).

One word of advice: don't attempt to unmould this when it's still hot, otherwise the rice will fall apart. Let it rest at room temperature for 15–20 minutes first – the cheese will still be melty and the rice warmed through. Of course, you can serve it at room temperature, too – you'll just have to forgo the 'stretchy cheese' factor.

1 quantity Ragù Abruzzese (see page 96)
150 g fresh or frozen peas
500 g carnaroli or arborio rice
100 g (1 cup) freshly grated parmigiano
1 egg, lightly beaten
salt flakes and freshly ground black pepper
30 g butter, melted
a few handfuls of dried breadcrumbs
100 g piece of salami, peeled and cut into small chunks
150 g provola cheese, cut into small cubes
4 hard-boiled eggs, peeled

SERVES 8

Make the ragù as instructed and stir through the peas. Set aside to cool.

Cook the rice in salted boiling water and drain a few minutes before it's al dente (so after about 12–13 minutes). Don't be afraid to leave it a little crunchy as it will keep cooking in the oven. Mix the rice with the ragù, add the parmigiano and beaten egg and stir thoroughly. Season to taste with salt and pepper.

Preheat your oven to 180°C.

Grease a bundt tin with the melted butter and coat the sides with breadcrumbs. Transfer half the rice mixture into the tin and create indents to accommodate the hard-boiled eggs, salami chunks and provola. Top with the remaining rice mixture, then level with a spoon and dust with some breadcrumbs.

Bake for 45–50 minutes or until golden. Remove from the oven and rest at room temperature for 15–20 minutes before unmoulding and slicing.

If you have some leftover sugo in your fridge or freezer, you could heat it up and serve it alongside the sliced timballo as a sauce.

THE TRUTH ABOUT RICE AND RISOTTO 131

Riso al salto (NEXT-DAY pan-fried risotto)

This is not a recipe. If you are Milanese, pan-fried rice is a way of life! In Milan we give the leftovers the same respect we give the risotto itself, because we know that those uneaten rice grains are going to be reborn with a crunchy, caramelised crust. In fact, when Mamma makes risotto, she always doubles the quantities to ensure riso al salto is on the menu the next day – it truly is that good. There's not much of a method, but I do have one important piece of advice for you: use a non-stick pan!

2 tablespoons extra-virgin olive oil
500 g leftover risotto (such as parmigiana or Milanese, see pages 116 and 118)
green salad, to serve

SERVES 4

Heat a 24 cm non-stick frying pan over medium–high heat, add the olive oil and swirl it around.

Add the leftover risotto and pat it down evenly with a wooden spoon. The idea is to create a 2 cm thick pancake, give or take.

Cook for 2–3 minutes or until you can see the edge caramelising. Slide it onto a plate, then quickly flip it back into the pan in one swift movement to colour the other side. If this maneuver feels a bit risky, turn your oven grill to high and slide the pan under the grill for 3–4 minutes or until the top is nicely caramelised. If you decide to use the grill option, make sure you use an ovenproof pan.

Cut into wedges and serve with a simple green salad.

Classic SICILIAN arancini

Some Italian dishes are so representative of our food culture that they need no introduction. This is definitely the case with the much-loved arancini, arguably the best thing to have ever happened to leftover rice! But of course, you don't have to go to the trouble of making risotto from scratch for the sole purpose of making arancini. If you are hit with a sudden craving, simply boil 350 g of carnaroli or arborio rice in salted water until al dente, drain and stir through 50 g (½ cup) of freshly grated parmigiano and 30 g of butter. Spread out on a plate to cool and set, then continue with the recipe below.

1 quantity Ragù Abruzzese
  (see page 96)
100 g fresh or frozen peas
salt flakes and freshly ground
  black pepper
500 g leftover risotto (such as
  parmigiana or Milanese,
  pages 116 and 118)
80 g provola cheese, cut into
  small chunks
200 g (1⅓ cups) plain flour
2 eggs, lightly beaten
200 g dried breadcrumbs
sunflower oil, for deep-frying

**MAKES 8–10 LARGE
ARANCINI**

Make the ragù as instructed, then let it simmer to reduce and thicken a little. Stir in the peas, then taste for salt and pepper and adjust accordingly. Set aside to cool completely at room temperature. (If you like, you can make the ragù the day before and keep it in the fridge.)

To assemble the arancini, it's important that both the risotto and ragù are cold.

Grab a handful of risotto and roll it into a ball the size of a large mandarin. (If the rice feels too dry, just keep squishing it with your hands until it feels nice and sticky.) Create a hollow in the middle, big enough to be stuffed with 1 tablespoon of ragù and a few pieces of provola. Grab a little extra risotto to seal the arancino, then give it a slight pear shape and set aside. Repeat with the remaining ingredients to make eight to ten arancini.

Place the flour, egg and breadcrumbs in separate shallow dishes.

Roll the arancini in flour, dusting off the excess. Dip them in the egg, letting the excess drip off, then roll in the breadcrumbs until coated. Place the arancini on a lined baking tray and chill for 30 minutes or until firm. They will keep in the fridge for 2–3 days or can be frozen and kept in an airtight container for up to 6 months.

Fill a deep-fryer or large saucepan with enough sunflower oil to fully submerge the arancini and heat to 180°C or until a cube of bread dropped in the oil browns in 15 seconds. Add the arancini in small batches and cook, turning halfway, for 3–4 minutes or until golden and crisp. Remove with a slotted spoon and drain on paper towel. Serve the arancini hot or at room temperature.

ANTIPASTO, grazing boards AND the SIMPLICITY OF ITALIAN gatherings

Italians love to entertain at home and no gathering is ever complete without antipasto, a tantalising appetiser to kick off the celebrations. It's often as simple as a snack of hand-cut salami with bread or house-baked olives and homemade grissini. At other times it's a more substantial affair, with grazing boards brimming with fruit, cheese, charcuterie and homemade bread (see note), which often replaces the main meal altogether. Think of it as the ultimate 'drink and nibbles' event, where everyone is encouraged to help themselves. It really takes the stress out of hosting as most of the prep is done in advance.

When the mood takes me, I like to cook a few simple yet impressive antipasto classics, such golden battered school prawns, mozzarella balls and zucchini strips served in a paper cone with a wedge of lemon. Give me that and a chilled Peroni and I am in heaven! Or how about deep-fried strips of dough that turn puffy and light as a feather the second they touch the hot oil, ready to be devoured with slices of mortadella and prosciutto? This is the best kind of finger food, sure to create a festive atmosphere and, most importantly, many happy memories.

The recipes in this chapter are representative of what Italians enjoy as antipasto. They range from flatbreads with cold cuts, homemade grissini and delightful gnocco fritto (the perfect offering for a share plate where nothing but a napkin is required), to dishes that are better suited to a sit-down meal. The sentiment behind each recipe is to keep it simple, a mantra in Italian home cooking. Even recipes that require actual cooking, such as frittata or baked zucchini flowers, involve very little labour and offer bucket loads of flavour in return.

Note: If you would like to add freshly baked bread or focaccia to your antipasto spread, see page 144 or 164 for some tasty ideas.

ANTIPASTO, grazing boards and the SIMPLICITY of ITALIAN gatherings

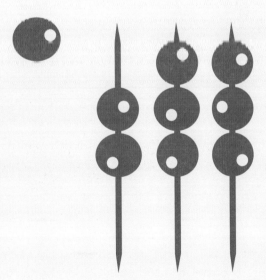

Crudo OF KINGFI/H WITH Campari AND orange DRE//ING

When an occasion calls for a sit-down meal one of my go-to antipasto dishes is a crudo of fish and pickled vegetables. It sounds very fancy and probably rather laborious, but it could not be easier or, most importantly, yummier. Crudo means raw in Italian, which immediately flags that this recipe requires no actual cooking, making it an all-time favourite in my kitchen.

Most reputable fishmongers sell sashimi-grade fish fillets these days, so shopping for ingredients is a walk in the park. And if your pantry is stocked with a few essentials such as sugar, vinegar and extra-virgin olive oil, and you have vegetables in the crisper that are in need of a face lift, this is the recipe for you.

Simply double the quantities if you'd like to serve this stunning dish as a main course.

125 ml (½ cup) white wine vinegar
3 tablespoons caster sugar
1 small fennel bulb, thinly sliced, fronds reserved
2–3 baby beetroots, thinly sliced
2 oranges
100 ml Campari
3 tablespoons extra-virgin olive oil
salt flakes and freshly ground black pepper
1 x 250 g sashimi-grade kingfish fillet

SERVES 4–6

Start by preparing the pickled vegetables. Heat the vinegar in a small saucepan over medium heat, add the sugar and simmer for 1–2 minutes or until it has dissolved. Divide the liquid evenly between two bowls, then add the fennel to one bowl and the beetroot to the other. Leave to pickle for at least 20 minutes and up to 24 hours (don't leave it any longer, otherwise the vibrant red of the beetroot will start to fade).

Peel and segment one orange, then finely chop three of the segments. (Reserve the remaining segments to scatter over the finished dish.) Squeeze the juice from the remaining orange into a bowl. Whisk together the Campari, olive oil, chopped orange segments and 2–3 tablespoons of the orange juice in a bowl. Season with salt and pepper and set aside.

Cut the fish into 3–4 mm thick slices. Arrange on a platter and dress with the Campari and orange dressing. Top with the pickled fennel and beetroot, the reserved orange segments and fennel fronds and some black pepper. Serve straight away or keep in the fridge until you're ready to serve (preferably within a few hours).

NOTES

This dish will also work just as well with other vegetables, such as carrots or celery. Give anything in your crisper that has gone a bit limp a glamorous makeover. And if you don't have the time to pickle your vegetables, store-bought ones are also fine.

I've used blood oranges here, but this dish will be delicious with whatever variety you can get your hands on.

Charcuterie board WITH homemade piadina

Piadina is a flatbread typical of the Emilia-Romagna region (the culinary epicentre of Italy), served with fillings like prosciutto and fontina, ham and pickled mushroom or a classic rocket, parmigiano and bresaola combo. It's easy to make at home as the dough doesn't need to rise, just a little beauty sleep to relax the gluten in the flour. Traditionally piadinas are made with shortening, but if that's not to your taste olive oil also gives spectacular results. This is a more 'deconstructed' version than classic piadina, as the flatbread is cut into wedges and the fillings are offered on the side, and for this reason it's perfectly suited to the informal nature of antipasto.

250 g (1⅔ cups) plain flour, plus extra for dusting
50 g vegetable shortening or 2½ tablespoons extra-virgin olive oil
125 ml (½ cup) milk
1 teaspoon salt flakes
mixed cold cuts and your choice of pickles and cheese, to serve

Combine the flour, shortening or olive oil, milk and salt in a large bowl. Turn out onto a floured surface and knead for 3–4 minutes. If the dough is a little dry, gradually add a little water and keep kneading until smooth.

Rest the dough in a floured bowl at room temperature for 30 minutes to allow the gluten in the flour to relax.

Cut the rested dough into quarters, then roll out each piece on a floured surface to a 2 mm thick round.

Heat a non-stick frying pan over medium heat. When warmed through, gently dry-fry one rolled piece of dough until the surface starts to bubble up. Flip it over and cook for another minute or until tiny blisters appear. Remove to a plate and cover to keep warm. Repeat with the remaining dough.

Cut the cooked piadina into wedges and serve with sliced meats, pickles and cheese.

Piadina will keep well wrapped in the fridge for 2–3 days. Alternatively, layer them between sheets of baking paper and freeze in an airtight container for up to 6 months.

BAKED zucchini FLOWERS with ricotta, MINT AND CHILLI

Zucchini flowers are often served coated in a crunchy batter, but when I'm entertaining at home I prefer to bake them. It means that I don't have to stand over a hot pan of scalding oil, frying in batches, and there is less pressure to eat them straight away, so I can relax and enjoy the company of my friends and family. The other advantage of baking them is that they are lighter and healthier, but still deliciously satisfying.

300 g fresh ricotta
3 tablespoons freshly grated
   pecorino
1 egg
3–4 mint leaves, finely chopped
pinch of freshly grated nutmeg
1 long red chilli, finely chopped
4–5 anchovy fillets, chopped
salt flakes
12 baby zucchini with their
   flowers, inner stamens
   removed
extra-virgin olive oil, for
   drizzling
crusty bread, to serve (optional)

SERVES 4

Preheat your oven to 200°C and line a baking tray with baking paper.

Combine the ricotta, pecorino, egg, mint, nutmeg, chilli and anchovy in a bowl. Taste for salt and adjust accordingly.

Gently open the petals of the zucchini flowers, spoon the ricotta mixture in and twist the petals to enclose. Place in a single layer on the prepared tray and drizzle with olive oil.

Bake for 20 minutes or until golden. Serve just as they are or with crusty bread, if you like.

The PERFECT bruschetta

You'll find bruschetta on most antipasto platters in Italy as it combines our four favourite ingredients: tomatoes, garlic, olive oil and bread! This is the traditional version and its disarming simplicity makes it a guaranteed crowd pleaser.

Great-quality olive oil is essential, so try and source a locally produced one that packs some pungency. Of course, summer tomatoes are also key, but it's not simply a matter of slicing them and arranging them on the bread. You must first rub the bread with garlic, then use the cut side of a tomato to smear tomato juice all over both sides of the bread before grilling it. This ensures that the tomato flavour permeates the crumb, creating a texture that is both crunchy (courtesy of the grilling) and fluffy. Once you have obtained a char that pleases you, top with chopped tomato and a liberal lick of extra-virgin olive oil, and they're ready to be devoured. I must warn you, it makes for messy eating, but it is so worth it!

Before you dive in, I need to clarify once and for all that the correct way to pronounce bruschetta is broos-ket-ah. Okay, go!

400 g mixed heirloom tomatoes
4 thick slices of sourdough (stale bread works really well, too)
2 garlic cloves, peeled and halved
salt flakes
3 tablespoons extra-virgin olive oil
basil leaves, to serve (optional)

SERVES 4

First, prepare the tomatoes. I usually slice some and roughly chop others, but remember to keep two larger tomatoes cut in half so you can smear the juice over the bread.

Rub the bread slices with the cut sides of the garlic cloves, then rub the cut side of the halved tomatoes onto both sides of the bread so they are dampened with the juices. Season with a little salt.

Heat a large chargrill pan over high heat. Add the bread slices and cook on both sides until charred to your liking.

Meanwhile, drizzle the olive oil over the remaining tomato and season with salt. Heap the tomato, juices and olive oil onto the grilled bread and season with a little more salt. Top with some basil leaves, if you like, and serve.

Neapolitan 'uoppo (GOLDEN fried bites)

Technically this is not a classic antipasto dish, it's more of a much-loved street food from Naples. If you ever venture there allow yourself to be guided by your nose, following the scent of 'uoppo (the abbreviation for 'cuoppo', a vernacular word for cup) cooking in the local 'friggitoria' (deep-fried food shop) like a hound tracking its prey! The reward is an unassuming paper cone filled to the brim with golden favourites such as bocconcini, zucchini flowers, prawns and other delights. All you need is a squeeze of lemon!

Serving this as an antipasto instantly creates a festive feel. Just make sure you hand out napkins as well! You can find paper cones in most party supply or specialty cookery shops, or online.

plain flour, for dusting
2 eggs, lightly beaten
500 g (5 cups) dried
  breadcrumbs
6 baby zucchini with their
  flowers, halved lengthways
1 small eggplant, cut lengthways
  into 1 cm thick strips
300 g school prawns, heads
  removed
1 lemon, well washed and cut
  into 5 mm thick rounds
8 bocconcini
sunflower oil, for deep-frying
salt flakes and freshly ground
  black pepper
lemon wedges, to serve

SERVES 4

Place the flour, egg and breadcrumbs in separate shallow dishes.

Dust the baby zucchini, eggplant, prawns, lemon slices and bocconcini with flour and shake off the excess. Dip them in the beaten egg, then roll in the breadcrumbs until evenly coated. (You may find the flour and breadcrumbs get a little messy, so you could start with half in the bowls, then replace it with the remaining flour and breadcrumbs halfway through.)

Pour sunflower oil into a large frying pan to a depth of at least 5 cm and heat to 180°C or until a cube of bread dropped in the oil browns in 15 seconds.

Working in batches, deep-fry the crumbed ingredients for about 2–3 minutes or until golden. Remove with a slotted spoon and drain on paper towel. Season with salt and pepper, and serve hot with lemon wedges on the side.

Gnocco FRITTO (Deep-fried DOUGH)

If you have travelled around Emilia-Romagna you would most likely have been introduced to the delights of gnocco fritto – strips of deep-fried dough so light and airy they defy the laws of physics. They are normally enjoyed as a starter with a selection of cold cuts and cheeses, the hollow interior offering the perfect home for a tasty filling. If shortening or lard isn't to your taste, you can use butter or olive oil instead.

1 teaspoon dried yeast
small pinch of caster sugar
400 g (2⅔ cups) plain or
   type '00' flour, plus extra
   for dusting
40 g vegetable shortening
   or lard
2 teaspoons salt flakes, plus
   extra to serve
vegetable oil, for deep-frying
your favourite cold cuts, pickles,
   olives and cheese, to serve

SERVES 8

Place the yeast, sugar and 180 ml (¾ cup) of water in a small bowl and stir until bubbly.

Tip the flour into a large bowl, add the yeast mixture and shortening or lard and start to mix together. Add the salt, then tip out onto a floured surface and knead for 3–4 minutes or until smooth.

Shape the dough into a ball, then place in a bowl and cover with a damp tea towel or beeswax wrap. Leave to prove in a warm place for 2 hours or until it has almost tripled in size.

Roll out the risen dough on a floured surface until 3–4 mm thick, then cut it into 5 cm x 5 cm diamond shapes.

Pour enough vegetable oil into a saucepan to come halfway up the side and heat over medium–high heat to 175°C or until a cube of bread dropped into the oil browns in about 20 seconds. Working in batches of four, drop in the diamond shapes and cook for a couple of minutes each side until golden. Remove with a slotted spoon and drain on paper towel.

Sprinkle the gnocco fritto with salt and serve hot with cold cuts of meat, pickles, olives and cheese.

Roasted chilli AND CRAB crostini

I have always been a summer person. When I was little I could hardly wait for the warmer months to come. They brought with them many of the things I held dear: the end of school, my birthday and relocating to my mamma's village in the heart of Abruzzo, far away from the chaos of city life in Milan.

A few decades may have gone by, but that little girl's excitement for summer remains unchanged. I happily absorb all the vitamin D I can get (ever mindful of sun damage … I've become so Australian!) as I potter around my garden and watch my crop of seasonal goodies come to life. I love chillies and have plenty growing in my garden, dotting the landscape with their vibrant green and red hues. I've made sure my children are as fond of them as my husband Richard and I are, as the thought of having to cook separate meals for them clashes deeply with my Italian upbringing.

If the people you are cooking for can't handle the heat of chilli, try roasting, peeling and seeding them. The flavours mellow beautifully, making them the perfect topping for this summer crostini – my ideal fuss-free crowd pleaser.

Crostini are very similar to bruschetta, but in Italy we only use that term for grilled bread rubbed with garlic and topped with tomatoes (in fact, the most traditional bruschetta simply has garlic and oregano!). Veer away from this classic combination and your preparation is instantly transformed into crostini. There is no particular reason for this; it is simply a matter of tradition and one I am happy to stick to.

10 large long red chillies
3 tablespoons chopped flat-leaf parsley leaves and chives
salt flakes
80 ml (⅓ cup) extra-virgin olive oil, plus extra for brushing
300 g picked crab meat
2 tablespoons lemon juice
2 garlic cloves, peeled and halved
1 day-old baguette, cut into 1 cm thick slices
small flat-leaf parsley leaves, to serve (optional)

SERVES 6

Preheat the grill function on your oven to high and line a baking tray with foil.

Place the chillies on the prepared tray, slide under the grill and roast, turning the chillies over as they blister, for 25–30 minutes or until blackened. Remove from the tray and place in a zip-lock bag for 1 hour.

Remove the chillies from the bag and scrape off the skin. Don't rinse them or you will wash away the beautiful charred flavour you've just given them. If you can't handle too much heat, scrape off the seeds. Cut the chillies into thin strips and mix with the chopped herbs, some salt and 2 tablespoons of the olive oil.

Place the crab meat in a small bowl and stir through the lemon juice and remaining olive oil.

Heat a chargrill pan over high heat or your barbecue grill plate to hot. Rub the cut sides of the garlic cloves over the bread slices, then brush with some more olive oil. Grill the bread on both sides until nicely charred. Top with the crab meat mixture and roasted chilli. Crown with a few small parsley leaves, if you like, and serve.

Homemade WALNUT grissini

Grissini are always a popular addition to an antipasto offering as they provide a welcome savoury flavour along with a wholesome, crunchy texture, especially if made with a combination of flours and extra ingredients like nuts. My advice is to double the quantities here as grissini are known to disappear the second they hit the table.

250 g (1⅔ cups) plain, type '00' or baker's flour, plus extra for dusting
150 g (1 cup) wholemeal flour
7 g sachet dried yeast
250 ml (1 cup) lukewarm water
3 tablespoons extra-virgin olive oil, plus extra for drizzling
1½ teaspoons salt flakes
60 g (½ cup) chopped walnuts

MAKES 16–18

Place the flours in a large bowl, add the yeast, water and 2 tablespoons of the olive oil and mix, then add the salt and continue mixing to bring the dough together. Tip onto a floured surface and knead for 2–3 minutes until smooth, then shape into a ball. Place in a floured bowl, then cover with a moist tea towel or beeswax wrap and leave to rest in a warm place for 20 minutes.

Remove the dough and stretch it into a rectangle. Fold the top and bottom thirds into the centre, like folding a letter, then tuck the ends under to form a ball. Place the dough back in the bowl, then cover and rest in a warm place for 1½–2 hours or until it has doubled in size.

Transfer the dough to a floured surface and shape into a rectangle. Sprinkle over two-thirds of the walnuts, then roll into a log. Cut the log into 16–18 pieces. Roll out and stretch each piece into a 25 cm long sausage. Using a pastry brush, coat the grissini with the remaining olive oil, then stud with the remaining walnuts.

Place the shaped grissini on a baking tray lined with baking paper, spaced apart to allow for more rising. Cover the tray with a damp tea towel or beeswax wrap and rest for 20 minutes.

Preheat your oven to 200°C.

Drizzle the grissini with a little extra olive oil and bake for 15 minutes or until golden and fragrant. Cool completely on a wire rack, then serve. These are best eaten on the day you make them.

NOTE
Pitted olives cut into small chunks also work beautifully as a flavouring.

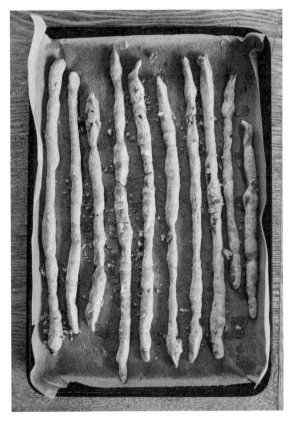

FRITTATA, TWO WAYS

Little squares or wedges of frittata make a wonderful addition to an antipasto platter. It is so versatile that it can be enjoyed in its barest form (beaten eggs, seasoning and a little grated parmigiano), or dressed up with fresh herbs and spring vegetables. I have learned a few tricks along the way from the Queen of Frittata herself (my mamma), a title bestowed on her by my husband, who goes weak at the knees whenever she starts beating eggs in a bowl!

Mamma never uses the oven; to retain maximum moisture, her frittata is always cooked in a hot pan over medium–high heat and masterfully flipped over. I concede it might be rather daunting to attempt this for the first time, but I swear to you, once you've got the knack you will never want to bake frittata in the oven again!

The Queen of Frittata's Rules

1. USE A NON-STICK PAN. Mamma always uses a medium-sized non-stick frying pan for an eight-egg frittata to make sure it retains some height once it's cooked. If you use a larger pan your frittata will look flat.

2. HEAT THE PAN THOROUGHLY. Make sure the pan is hot before you add the oil, then swirl it around to evenly coat the base and side of the pan.

3. DROP IN THE EGG MIXTURE ALL AT ONCE. Don't be shy. Drop it in and immediately swirl to spread it out evenly. As it starts to set, move it gently with a spatula to allow the liquid mixture to get in contact with the base of the pan. When it looks like it's three quarters set, arrange the vegetables on top, then cover with a lid for 1 minute.

4. FLIP THE FRITTATA. To do this safely, slide the frittata onto a large plate, wet-side up. Place the pan over the plate, then in one swift and decisive move, flip the plate over to transfer the frittata back to the pan. Return the pan to the heat.

5. KEEP IT SHORT AND SWEET. Once you've flipped the frittata, cook it for just 30 seconds, then immediately turn it onto a plate or board. If you leave it in the hot pan it will dry out. If you're adding herbs, let the frittata cool first, otherwise they will wilt and turn brown.

6. CHOOSE YOUR INGREDIENTS WISELY. Of course you can add whatever you like in the quantities you crave, but because this is a book about authentic Italian home cooking, I feel compelled to clarify that not all ingredients are suited to frittata. You will never catch an Italian home cook adding raw garlic, raw onion, pumpkin, sweet potato, feta, chicken, lamb, beef, pork or fish (although an exception can be made for crab!), raw capsicum, pesto, haloumi or baked beans. Our credo is 'keep it simple', so the classic Italian frittata additions are fried zucchini, stewed onion, cooked potato, foraged wild greens and asparagus.

7. MILK IT. Whether to add milk to the egg mixture is the subject of some controversy. Those who do it fervently believe it adds a fluffy texture; those who don't simply dismiss the idea with a smirk. Naturally I have to follow the rules of the Queen herself, and therefore side with the milk faction.

NOTE: Frittata is often served as a main meal. If you would like to do that, allow two eggs per person.

Spring FRITTATA WITH baby asparagus, mint AND chives

The combination of eggs and asparagus is a timeless springtime classic. These verdant spears enjoy a fairly short season and as soon as they appear on the market I become obsessed with their bright, earthy flavour, and turn them into the hero ingredient of just about everything I make!

1 bunch of baby asparagus, woody ends trimmed
8 eggs, lightly beaten
3 tablespoons milk
3 tablespoons freshly grated pecorino or parmigiano
2 tablespoons chopped chives, plus extra to serve (optional)
salt flakes and freshly ground black pepper
80 ml (⅓ cup) extra-virgin olive oil
mint leaves, to serve

SERVES 8–10

Blanch the asparagus in a saucepan of salted boiling water for 2 minutes. Drain and refresh under cold water, then set aside.

Mix the egg, milk, grated cheese and chives in a large bowl. Season well with salt and pepper.

Heat a medium non-stick frying pan over medium–high heat until nice and hot, then add the olive oil and swirl to evenly coat the base and side. Drop in the egg mixture and swirl to spread it out evenly. As the egg starts to set, move it slightly with a spatula to allow the liquid mixture to get in contact with the base of the pan.

When the egg mixture looks like it's three-quarters set, arrange the asparagus on top. Cover with a lid and cook for 1 minute, then slide the frittata onto a plate and flip it back into the pan (see instructions on page 159). Cook for 30 seconds, then flip the frittata onto a plate so that the asparagus is on top again and allow to cool slightly.

Top with mint leaves and extra chives (if using) just before serving, then cut into squares or wedges and enjoy. Any leftovers can be eaten fridge cold the next day.

Frittata with stewed SHALLOTS

Mamma's frittata con scalogni (frittata with shallots) is one of the best uses of these small onions, gently stewed in good olive oil, salt and a touch of balsamic until they surrender their natural sweetness. A classic antipasto dish.

80 ml (⅓ cup) extra-virgin olive oil
5 golden shallots, thinly sliced
salt flakes and freshly ground black pepper
2 tablespoons balsamic vinegar
8 eggs, lightly beaten
3 tablespoons milk

SERVES 8–10

Heat 2 tablespoons of the olive oil in a medium non-stick frying pan over medium heat, add the shallot and a pinch of salt and cook for 3–4 minutes. Add a splash of water if the shallot starts sticking to the base of the pan. Pour in the balsamic vinegar and cook for a further 2–3 minutes or until the shallot is soft and caramelised. Season with salt and pepper, then transfer to a plate and set aside.

Wipe out the pan and heat it over medium–high heat.

Meanwhile, mix the egg and milk in a large bowl. Season well with salt and pepper.

Add the remaining olive oil to the pan and swirl to evenly coat the base and side. Drop in the egg mixture and swirl to spread it out evenly. As it starts to set, move it slightly with a spatula to allow the liquid mixture to get in contact with the base of the pan.

When the egg mixture looks like it's three-quarters set, arrange the shallot mixture on top. Cover with a lid and cook for 1 minute, then slide the frittata onto a plate and flip it back into the pan (see instructions on page 159). Cook for 30 seconds, then slide the frittata onto a plate to cool slightly.

Cut into squares or wedges and enjoy. Any leftovers can be eaten fridge cold the next day.

Focaccia PUGLIEJE

This stunning focaccia from the Apulian region of Italy (the heel) is famous for its ineffable lightness and bounce. The recipe uses a very clever ingredient to make the dough so soft: boiled and mashed potatoes! The resulting texture is incredibly airy and spongy. The Pugliesi top it with their sun-ripened cherry tomatoes, piquant olive oil and oregano, and consume this delicacy with equal enthusiasm for breakfast, lunch or merenda (afternoon tea). Adding this to your antipasto spread is sure to make you very popular with your lucky friends and family.

500 g (3⅓ cups) plain or type '00' flour, plus extra if needed and for dusting
7 g sachet dried yeast
2½ tablespoons extra-virgin olive oil, plus extra for drizzling
150 ml milk, plus extra if needed
300 g potatoes, boiled, peeled, mashed and cooled
salt flakes
cherry tomatoes and dried oregano, for topping

SERVES 6–8

Place the flour and yeast in a large bowl, add the olive oil, milk, mashed potato and 100 ml of water and mix until it comes together. Season with a generous pinch of salt, then tip onto a floured surface and knead for 2–3 minutes or until smooth. If the dough is a bit dry, add a little more milk or water; if it's too wet, add a little extra flour.

Cover the bowl with a damp tea towel and allow to rise at room temperature for 2 hours or until doubled in size.

Preheat your oven to 200°C and line a baking tray with baking paper.

Place the dough on the prepared tray and gently stretch with floured hands to a rectangle about 1 cm thick. Top with halved or whole cherry tomatoes, dried oregano, salt and a little extra olive oil and bake for 20–25 minutes or until golden and puffed up.

ROASTS, braises AND second COURSES

One lesser known fact about Italian home cooking is that we hardly ever indulge in multiple-course meals. More often than not we are content with either a bowl of pasta or what we refer to as 'secondo' (second course), which is normally protein based. I hear your confusion here: if pasta is a 'primo' (first) and meat or fish is a secondo, which one is the main course? The simple answer is that they both are. I know I am probably not making this any easier to understand! If we were to define the culinary habits of Italians by the way we are represented in movies and literature, it appears that we normally consume two main courses at each meal. The simple truth is that we only sit around lavish tables brimming with multiple courses on special occasions or perhaps for Sunday lunch. Our everyday eating habits are much simpler, and possibly healthier, than some may think.

In this chapter I have included ten of my favourite non-pasta-based meals, some passed on to me by my mother and others that I have picked up along the way. The common thread is simplicity. You won't find recipes with myriad ingredients here; most of them are just pantry staples with a few fresh, seasonal items.

I encourage you to browse through this chapter for inspiration, and then create your own versions, adding your personal touches along the way. And if you are looking at lip-smackingly delicious sides to serve with them, there is a whole chapter of ideas on page 193.

Of course, if the mood takes you or you are having a special celebration day, go all out! Start with an antipasto, followed by a pasta (or gnocchi or risotto) and then a second course with vegetables, and you can be assured you will be serving your food with a large side of happiness!

ROASTS, braises and SECOND COURSES

Vegetable TIELLA

Preparing this impressive-looking dish is as easy as slicing some vegetables. After that, all you need to do is arrange the discs in pretty concentric circles and drizzle them with plenty of olive oil; after an hour in the oven your kitchen will smell like a terrace in the Cinque Terre! This is a fabulous vegan main meal, which, of course, can also be served as a side dish.

2–3 Japanese eggplants, cut into 1 cm thick rounds
3–4 zucchini, cut into 1 cm thick rounds
6–7 roma tomatoes, cut into 1 cm thick rounds
2 golden shallots, cut into 5 mm thick slices
3 tablespoons extra-virgin olive oil, plus extra for drizzling
salt flakes and freshly ground black pepper
3–4 garlic cloves, skin on, smashed with the back of a knife
40 g (½ cup) fresh breadcrumbs

SERVES 6

Preheat your oven to 200°C.

Place the eggplant, zucchini, tomato and shallot in a bowl, add the olive oil and some salt and pepper and toss to combine.

Oil a 30 cm round baking dish. Arrange alternate slices of eggplant, zucchini, tomato and shallot in the dish, standing them upright. Scatter the garlic over the top, drizzle with a little extra olive oil and bake for 35–40 minutes or until fragrant and lightly golden.

Sprinkle over the breadcrumbs, drizzle with a little extra olive oil and season with more salt. Bake for a further 15 minutes or until crispy.

Serve warm or at room temperature. If you like, you can squeeze the softened garlic cloves out of their skins and onto the tiella.

SICILIAN eggplant ROLLS

This dish of grilled eggplant slices stuffed with ricotta and baked in a pool of tomatoes is a phenomenal vegetarian main course. Its flavour profile references the Arab domination of Sicily, with ingredients such as nutmeg and sultanas added to the Italian classics.

It's wonderful scalding hot from the oven, just as delicious warm and surprisingly satisfying fridge cold, perfect for a midnight snack after a big night out, or when you come home famished after a hard session at the gym.

If you are making this a day ahead, assemble the rolls in the sauce without baking, then the next day put the cheese on top and bake as instructed.

2 large eggplants, cut lengthways into 5 mm thick slices (you should end up with about 14 slices)
2 tablespoons extra-virgin olive oil
1 quantity Sugo (see page 28)
150 g fresh mozzarella, torn into small pieces
3–4 tablespoons freshly grated pecorino
3 tablespoons pine nuts (optional)
freshly ground black pepper
basil leaves, to serve

RICOTTA FILLING
1 tablespoon extra-virgin olive oil
1 garlic clove, skin on, bashed with the back of a knife
1 bunch of silverbeet, stalks removed and finely chopped, leaves roughly chopped
500 g fresh ricotta, well drained
30 g (⅓ cup) freshly grated pecorino
1 egg
2–3 tablespoons chopped flat-leaf parsley leaves
¼ teaspoon freshly grated nutmeg
2 tablespoons sultanas, soaked in water for 30 minutes, drained
salt flakes and freshly ground black pepper

SERVES 4

Heat a large chargrill pan over high heat. Brush the eggplant slices with the olive oil, then grill for about 3–4 minutes on both sides until they are soft and have nice, dark char lines.

Preheat your oven to 200°C.

While the oven is heating, make the ricotta filling. Heat the olive oil in a frying pan over high heat, add the garlic, then drop in the chopped silverbeet stalks. Cover and cook for 2 minutes or until softened. Add the silverbeet leaves, replace the lid and leave for 1–2 minutes until wilted. Drain off the excess liquid and discard the garlic clove. Mix the cooked silverbeet with the remaining ingredients in a bowl and season with salt and pepper.

To assemble, smear a ladleful of the sugo over the base of a baking dish. Put 1 tablespoon of the ricotta filling in the middle of each eggplant slice and roll up to enclose.

Arrange the rolls, seam-side down, in a single layer in the dish. Drizzle the remaining sugo over the top. Scatter over the mozzarella and pecorino and bake for 25–30 minutes or until golden and bubbling. Remove and rest at room temperature for 5 minutes before serving.

In the meantime, if you'd like to use pine nuts to top the dish, heat a small non-stick frying pan over medium heat and toast the pine nuts for 45–60 seconds until fragrant and lightly golden. Sprinkle over the eggplant.

To serve, grind over some black pepper and top with plenty of basil.

ROASTED TIGER prawns with olives, tomatoes AND CRISPY CRUMBS

Nothing says Mediterranean summer more than salty seafood, sun-ripened tomatoes and juicy olives. Add a touch of chilli and crunchy breadcrumbs, and you will be day-dreaming about sipping pinot grigio on the Amalfi Coast! Luckily, food is a beautiful way to travel from the comfort of your kitchen. Just get yourself the freshest prawns you can find and you'll have your own taste of la dolce vita!

4–5 tablespoons Ligurian olives (available at delis)
600 g cherry or heirloom tomatoes, halved
1 tablespoon finely chopped flat-leaf parsley stalks
1–2 long red chillies, halved lengthways
80 ml (⅓ cup) extra-virgin olive oil
2 garlic cloves
salt flakes
12 tiger prawns
2 slices of stale sourdough
2 tablespoons chopped flat-leaf parsley leaves, plus extra to serve (optional)

SERVES 4

Preheat your oven to 180°C and grease a large roasting tin with olive oil.

Remove the pits from the olives by pressing them on a board, either with the palm of your hand or using a glass or a cup. Place the olives in a bowl, add the tomato, parsley stalk, chilli and 2 tablespoons of the olive oil. Take one garlic clove (skin on) and bash it with the back of a knife. Add to the bowl, then season with salt and toss everything together. Tip the mixture into the prepared tin, spread it out in a single layer and roast for 25 minutes.

Meanwhile, prepare the prawns. Remove the heads and freeze for later use (they make great fish stock). Peel and devein the prawns, but keep the tails attached. Brush them with a little of the remaining olive oil.

Take the tin out of the oven, place the prawns on the tomato mixture and season them with salt. Roast for another 6–8 minutes or until the prawns are just cooked through.

In the meantime, place the stale bread in a food processor. Peel the remaining garlic clove and add to the processor, along with the parsley leaves and a good pinch of salt. Blitz to form coarse breadcrumbs with some bigger chunks of bread remaining.

Heat the remaining olive oil in a frying pan over high heat and fry the breadcrumb mixture, stirring often, until golden and fragrant. Scatter the breadcrumbs over the roasted prawns and tomatoes, top with some extra parsley, if you like, and serve.

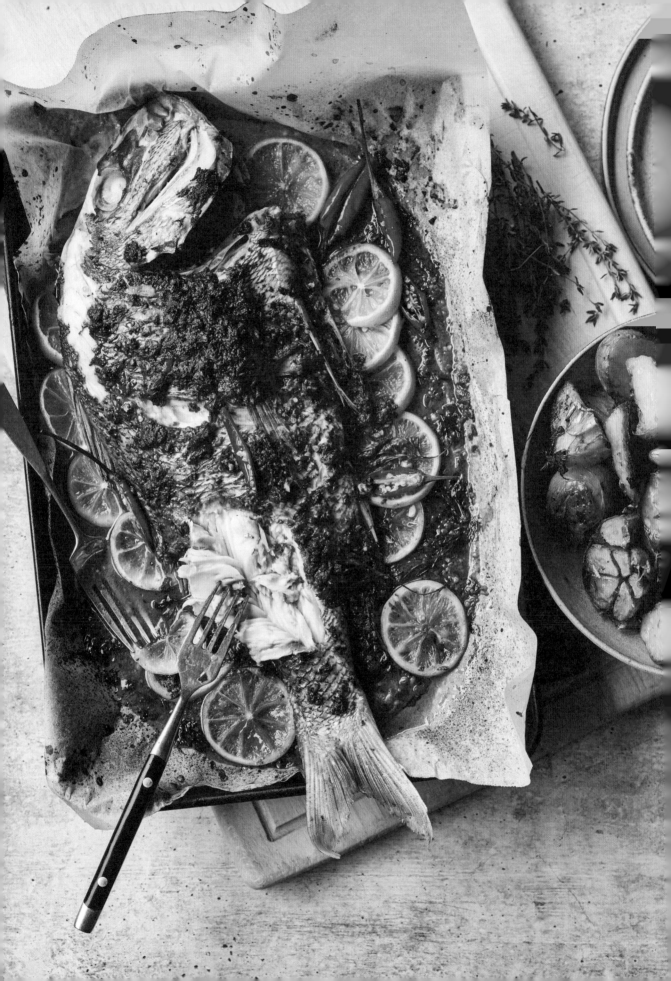

Whole ROASTED snapper with chilli, lemon, olives AND capers

If you've never felt confident enough to cook a whole fish, then let me introduce you to one of my favourite, incredibly easy recipes! All you need to do is source a beautiful snapper (males are tastier than females – just look for the hump on the head) and ask your fishmonger to scale and gut it for you. When you get home, simply whiz up a few ingredients, unceremoniously slap them onto the fish and put it in the oven. One glass of wine later your dinner will be ready!

4–5 chillies (any type is fine), plus extra for roasting (optional)
60 g (⅓ cup) capers in salt, rinsed and drained
a few handfuls of black pitted olives (or as many as you like)
1 small bunch of flat-leaf parsley, roughly chopped
4 garlic cloves, peeled
80 ml (⅓ cup) extra-virgin olive oil
80 ml (⅓ cup) white wine
1 large whole snapper, scaled and gutted
1 lemon, thinly sliced
salt flakes
Balsamic Roast Potatoes (see page 208), to serve (optional)

SERVES 4–6

Preheat your oven to 200°C and line a large baking tray with baking paper.

Put the chillies, capers, olives, parsley and 1 garlic clove in a food processor and whiz to a paste. Gradually add half the olive oil and half the wine to loosen it.

Score the snapper a few times on each side. Place it on the prepared tray, then spread the paste on both sides of the fish. Arrange the lemon slices around the snapper on the tray, as well as the extra chillies for roasting (if using). Season with salt and drizzle over the remaining olive oil and wine.

Roast for 20–25 minutes or until the fish is just cooked through. The flesh should be just firm and white, but ever so slightly translucent closer to the bone.

Serve with the crispy lemon slices on the side and balsamic roast potatoes, if desired.

GRILLED BABY octopus with kipfler potato salad

My mamma's secret to succulent octopus is to gently poach it before introducing it to the hot flames. This first step is essential to achieve that melt-in-the-mouth texture and avoid any chewiness. The poaching liquid itself becomes an intensely flavoured nectar and can be used as a dressing for the octopus and waxy kipfler potatoes. Of course, don't forget the olive oil. Ever!

1 kg baby octopus (ask your fishmonger to clean them for you)
600 g kipfler potatoes, skin on, well scrubbed
3 tablespoons extra-virgin olive oil, plus extra for drizzling
2 spring onions, thinly sliced
2–3 tablespoons chopped chives
salt flakes and freshly ground black pepper

POACHING LIQUID
2 tablespoons extra-virgin olive oil
1 dried chilli, chopped
1 garlic clove, sliced
100 ml white wine
2 bay leaves

SERVES 4

Combine all the poaching liquid ingredients in a heavy-based saucepan, add the baby octopus and bring to a simmer. Reduce the heat to low, then cover and gently poach for 1 hour or until fork tender. Set aside and let the octopus cool in its liquid. Don't discard the liquid!

Boil the potatoes in their skins until tender, then drain and cut into bite-sized chunks. Toss the potato with the olive oil, spring onion, chives and 2 tablespoons of the reserved poaching liquid, and season with salt and pepper.

Heat your barbecue grill plate to hot.

Drain the octopus and pat dry, then grill on both sides until nicely charred. This should only take a few minutes. Season with salt, then drizzle with a little extra oil and 1–2 tablespoons of the poaching liquid. Serve warm or at room temperature with the potato salad.

Cacciucco (TUSCAN fish ZUPPA)

Of the many types of fish stews typical of Italy, cacciucco is a favourite of mine for a few reasons. Firstly, it is uncomplicated to make, yet looks and tastes stunning, which makes it a winner for both family dinners and more formal occasions. Secondly, I love the way old recipe books indicate that you need to have the same number of seafood varieties as there are letter Cs in cacciucco: five, to be precise! And while the choice of fish is largely the cook's privilege, the unspoken rule is that at least one should be a spiny fish, such as scorpion fish or red mullet. These can be tricky to come by, so I have used ling here. I hope my Tuscan friends can forgive this transgression!

3 tablespoons extra-virgin olive oil
2 garlic cloves, finely chopped
2 tablespoons finely chopped flat-leaf parsley leaves, plus extra leaves to serve
100 ml white wine
2 x 400 g cans chopped tomatoes
1 litre fish stock
300 g skinless ling or barramundi fillet, pin-boned, cut into 3 cm pieces
12 large raw prawns, peeled and deveined, tails intact
8 scallops, roe removed
8 mussels, scrubbed and debearded (see note)
8 clams, rinsed
grilled bread, to serve

SERVES 4

Heat the olive oil in a large saucepan over medium–high heat, add the garlic and parsley and cook, stirring, for 1–2 minutes until fragrant. Pour in the wine and cook for a further 2–3 minutes until the wine has evaporated. Add the chopped tomatoes and stock and bring to a simmer, then reduce the heat to medium–low and cook for 20–30 minutes until reduced and slightly thickened.

Add the fish and prawns and cook for 1 minute, then add the remaining seafood. Cover and cook, shaking the pan once or twice, for a further 1–2 minutes until the mussels and clams have opened (discard any that don't open) and all the seafood is cooked through. Ladle into bowls and serve with plenty of grilled bread.

NOTE
To remove the beards from your mussels, tug the little hairy bit away from its base. The beards are not inedible, but they are definitely not very palatable.

CHICKEN diavola

Diavola in Italian means 'devil's style' but its association with Satan has nothing to do with how many sins one may be guilty of, and everything to do with its fiery hot flavour. Use as many chillies as you can handle, but please be careful when you chop them – either use gloves or wash your hands immediately afterwards. This advice comes from a very clumsy cook who has often forgotten to do so and then rubbed her eyes!

2 x 1.2–1.5 kg chickens, spatchcocked (see note)
salt flakes and freshly ground black pepper
100 ml extra-virgin olive oil
125 ml (½ cup) dry white wine
5–6 bird's eye chillies, cut into chunks
1–2 handfuls of fresh herbs (such as marjoram, rosemary and oregano)
3–4 garlic cloves, skin on, bashed with the back of a knife
2 small onions, peeled and halved
1 lemon, cut into slices

SERVES 8

Preheat your oven to 220°C.

Place the chickens in a large roasting tin and season well with salt and pepper.

Mix the olive oil, white wine, chilli and herbs in a jug, then pour evenly over the chickens. Scatter the garlic, onion halves and lemon slices into the tin, then roast for 45–50 minutes until the chickens are cooked through and golden brown on top. Remove and rest at room temperature for 10–15 minutes before carving.

Serve with your favourite side dish and plenty of Sangiovese wine.

NOTE
You can ask your butcher to spatchcock your chickens for you. Or, if you feel brave enough, you can try it yourself – simply cut off the neck bone with kitchen scissors, then crush the spine with your hands.

ROMAN-STYLE braised chicken

This dish is as quintessentially Roman as the expression 'mortacci tua' (damn you!). The chicken cooks ever so gently on a bed of tomatoes, sweet shallots and capsicum. Enjoying this trattoria classic without plenty of bread to mop up the glorious sauce is almost criminal, so if you don't want me to yell Roman vernacular swear words at you, make sure you have a large loaf at the ready, or, at the very least, some mashed potatoes!

80 ml (⅓ cup) extra-virgin olive oil
4 chicken marylands
4 golden shallots, thinly sliced
salt flakes and freshly ground black pepper
2 garlic cloves, skin on, bashed with the back of a knife
2 red and 2 yellow capsicums, deseeded and cut into 5 mm thick strips
150 ml white wine
500 ml (2 cups) Quick and Easy Passata (see page 29)
1 litre chicken stock
handful of baby capers, rinsed and drained
basil leaves, to serve
Olive Oil Mashed Potatoes (see page 196) or crusty bread, to serve

SERVES 4

Heat the olive oil in a large heavy-based saucepan over medium–high heat. Add the chicken and cook on both sides for 3–4 minutes until golden. Lift out the chicken and set aside.

Add the shallot to the pan, season with a pinch of salt and cook, stirring, for a few minutes to soften, then add the garlic and capsicum and mix well. Return the chicken to the pan and deglaze with the wine, scraping up any bits caught on the base. Simmer for 2–3 minutes to allow the alcohol to evaporate. Pour in the passata and stock and bring to a simmer, then season with salt. Reduce the heat to low, cover and cook gently for 20–25 minutes or until the chicken is cooked through.

Remove the lid, then transfer the chicken to a plate and set aside. Increase the heat and cook the sauce for a further 25–30 minutes until reduced and thickened. Taste and adjust the seasoning if necessary, then discard the garlic cloves and return the chicken to the pan to heat through. Remove from the heat and stir in the baby capers.

Arrange the chicken on a platter and cover liberally with the sauce. Finish with a generous grinding of black pepper and basil leaves, and serve with mashed potato or crusty bread.

Ligurian LAMB SHANKS

I often turn to this dish when I have friends over for Sunday lunch and they always ask what the secret is to such a beautiful dish. Of course, it is hugely tempting to blow my own trumpet and hint at the hours I spent slaving away in the kitchen, but in truth, the real secret to this dish is time management. You need to allow a good three hours of cooking time, but don't worry, the only real labour takes about ten minutes. That's a pretty sweet deal, considering your reward at the end is fall-from-the-bone tender meat, swimming in a thick broth enriched with wine, lemon and thyme. Knives are redundant here, though bread certainly comes in handy to mop up the extra sauce.

4 French-trimmed lamb shanks
3 tablespoons plain flour
80 ml (⅓ cup) extra-virgin olive oil
salt flakes and freshly ground black pepper
3 garlic cloves, skin on, bashed with the back of a knife
1 red onion, thinly sliced
1 carrot, roughly chopped
1 celery stalk, roughly chopped
3 thyme sprigs, plus extra leaves to serve
180 ml (¾ cup) white wine
500 ml (2 cups) chicken or beef stock
3 desiree potatoes (about 600 g in total), peeled and cut into wedges
100 g (¾ cup) pitted mixed olives
finely grated zest of 1 lemon
2–3 tablespoons toasted pine nuts

SERVES 4

Dust the lamb shanks in the flour, shaking off the excess.

Heat 2 tablespoons of the olive oil in a large flameproof casserole dish over medium–high heat. Season the lamb, then add to the dish and cook, turning, for 6–8 minutes until nicely browned all over. Remove and set aside.

Reduce the heat to medium, add the garlic, onion, carrot, celery, thyme and remaining oil and cook for 2–3 minutes until fragrant. Return the lamb to the dish and season with salt and pepper. Increase the heat to high and deglaze with the white wine, scraping up any bits caught on the base. Cook for 1–2 minutes until the alcohol has evaporated. Pour in the stock and enough water to cover the lamb, then reduce the heat to low and cook, covered, for 2 hours.

Add the potato and olives, then put the lid back on and cook for another 45 minutes or until the lamb is very tender and the potato is cooked through. Remove the lid and simmer for 10–15 minutes until the liquid has reduced by one third. Take off the heat and season with salt and pepper.

Sprinkle the lemon zest, pine nuts and extra thyme leaves over the lamb shanks and serve.

Mamma's BEEF spezzatino WITH borlotti beans

I grew up in Milan, which is known for its long, cold and foggy winters. For a summer girl like me, those gloomy months used to be rather challenging. Lucky for me, Mamma had an arsenal of winter warmers to sustain us throughout the season, making the thought of coming home from school a little sweeter. This is a variation on her classic beef stew with potatoes, with the addition of creamy borlotti beans. Utter magnificence!

500 g dried borlotti beans, soaked in water overnight, drained (see note)
5 potatoes, scrubbed
3–4 bay leaves
salt flakes and freshly ground black pepper
80 ml (⅓ cup) extra-virgin olive oil
4 beef cheeks
plain flour (or rice flour for a gluten-free option), for dredging
50 g piece of smoked pancetta
1 onion, finely chopped
2 carrots, finely chopped
2 celery stalks, finely chopped
200 ml red wine
2 x 400 g cans chopped tomatoes
flat-leaf parsley leaves, to serve
crusty bread, to serve

SERVES 4

Fill a large saucepan with water, add the drained beans, one whole potato and a bay leaf (no salt) and simmer for 1 hour or until the beans are cooked through. Let the beans cool in the liquid, then drain and discard the bay leaf and potato. Season with salt and set aside.

Meanwhile, heat 3 tablespoons of the olive oil in a large flameproof casserole dish over medium heat. Dredge the beef cheeks in flour, shaking off the excess, then brown on all sides for 2–3 minutes. Season with salt, then lift them out and set aside.

Add the remaining oil to the dish, along with the pancetta, onion, carrot and celery, and cook, stirring, until caramelised. Return the cheeks to the dish. Deglaze with the red wine, scraping up any bits caught on the base, and cook for 3–4 minutes until the alcohol has evaporated. Add the tomatoes, remaining bay leaves and enough water to cover completely, then season with salt and bring to a simmer. Reduce the heat to low, then cover and cook gently for 2–3 hours or until the meat starts to fall apart.

Peel the remaining potatoes, cut them into wedges and add to the dish. Cover and cook for a further 40 minutes. Remove the lid, add the beans and cook over medium heat for 10 minutes to allow the excess liquid to reduce slightly. Taste for salt and adjust if needed. Finish with a grinding of pepper and parsley leaves and serve with crusty bread.

NOTE
If you are using fresh borlotti beans, simply pod them and add them to the dish with the potatoes.

SIDE dishes take CENTRE STAGE

It was quite a task to select only a small number of recipes for this chapter. We adore our vegetables in Italy and reserve a very special place for them in our daily diet, often consumed as sides, or sometimes as a frugal meal, accompanied by chunks of bread.

Our love for the fruits of our soil extends to tubers, particularly potatoes, which occupy an illustrious seat in the spotlight. I had to stop myself at four potato recipes, but I could have kept on going, such is my devotion to this humble vegetable.

When cooking Italian sides, my best advice is to have your olive oil on hand, as we tend to favour it over butter. That said, because I cannot ignore my northern Italian upbringing I also share a family favourite of braised fennel, baked in lashings of both butter and milk, a total dairy extravaganza!

Use this chapter as you wish: pick a few dishes to serve with a second course (see page 167), or simply enjoy them on their own for a spectacular vegetarian or vegan meal.

SIDE dishes take CENTRE STAGE

Olive OIL mashed potatoes

It is a well-known truth that Italians adore their olive oil and it's pretty obvious that I am no exception. I use it in most of my cooking, both sweet and savoury, frequently replacing butter with this emerald green nectar. I particularly love the grassy notes it adds to mashed potatoes, and often use a pungent Tuscan-style extra-virgin olive oil for added flavour. If you swap dairy milk for nut milk, this lovely side dish becomes vegan friendly, too.

700 g red potatoes, skin on
80 ml (⅓ cup) extra-virgin
   olive oil
150 ml warm milk
salt flakes and freshly ground
   white or black pepper

SERVES 4

Fill a saucepan with cold salted water, drop in the potatoes and simmer over medium–high heat for 25–30 minutes or until tender. Drain well, then peel the potatoes and pass them through a potato ricer or mash with a masher while still hot.

Add the olive oil and three-quarters of the warm milk and beat well with a wooden spoon. Add a little more milk if it is too thick. Season to taste with salt and pepper and serve.

VERDURE ripassate (GREENS WITH garlic AND chilli)

In Italy 'ripassati' means sauteed in garlic, chilli and olive oil – the holy trinity of Italian cooking. You can pretty much 'ripassare' most greens that require a little cooking, such as chicory, escarole, kale, broccoli rabe, broccolini and, my personal favourite, cavolo nero (Tuscan kale). All you need to do is season it well and finish with a squeeze of lemon.

2 bunches of cavolo nero
3 tablespoons extra-virgin
  olive oil
2 garlic cloves, skin on, bashed
  with the back of a knife
1 bird's eye chilli or 1 dried chilli,
  finely chopped
pinch of salt flakes
a little squeeze of lemon juice
crusty bread and cheese,
  to serve

SERVES 4

Remove and discard the middle ribs from the cavolo nero leaves, then cut each leaf into three or four pieces. Blanch them in a large saucepan of salted boiling water for 1 minute, then drain well.

Heat the olive oil in a frying pan over medium–low heat, add the garlic and chilli and cook for 1–2 minutes or until softened.

Add the cavolo nero to the frying pan, and toss over medium heat for 1 minute or until the greens are nicely coated in the chilli and garlic oil. Season with a good pinch of salt and squeeze over a little lemon juice. Serve as a side dish or by itself, with some bread and cheese.

ZUCCHINI *scapece* (Fried zucchini WITH vinegar AND mint)

When zucchini are in season they are a permanent feature in my kitchen, and the kitchens of many other Italian home cooks, as they are so versatile and suit practically any preparation. They are gorgeous left raw and thinly sliced in salads, stuffed with ricotta and herbs and baked until golden, or simply cut into rounds, fried and then marinated in vinegar (scapece style), like they do in Naples. It's a dish that benefits from some resting time, to allow all the flavours to mingle harmoniously, and its 'make ahead' vibe suits the busy lifestyles of families perfectly. Serve it as an antipasto (see page 137 for ideas) or as a side dish to fish, and your day will be immeasurably brighter and tastier!

extra-virgin olive oil, for
    shallow-frying
2 garlic cloves, skin on, bashed
    with the back of a knife
6 zucchini, cut into 5 mm
    thick rounds
3 tablespoons red wine vinegar
3 tablespoons white wine
    vinegar
small handful of mint leaves
salt flakes

SERVES 4

Pour 3 cm of olive oil into a frying pan and heat over medium heat. Fry the garlic for 30 seconds, then remove with a slotted spoon and drain on paper towel.

Working in two or three batches, fry the zucchini rounds for 3 minutes or until cooked and nicely browned on both sides. Remove and drain on paper towel.

Combine the vinegars in a small jug. Place the zucchini, garlic and half the mint in a bowl, then pour over the vinegar mixture and toss to combine. Season with salt to taste and leave to marinate for 2–3 hours.

Drain off the excess liquid, then place the zucchini in a serving dish and top with the remaining mint.

NOTE
The name 'scapece' is a hangover from a bygone era when southern Italy was under Spanish invasion. 'Escabeche' is Spanish for pickled, and 'scapece' has since become its Neapolitan vernacular translation.

Mediter-ranean POTATOES

This colourful dish is the epitome of Mediterranean cuisine. A wonderful concoction of all the classic ingredients that so eloquently speak of our climate and palate, such as tomatoes, capers, olives, garlic, wine and chilli. As the potato cubes roast, they absorb all those precious flavours like thirsty sponges, turning into golden nuggets of pure delight. Any leftovers are excellent the next day for a quick pasta dish.

500 g cherry tomatoes, halved
5 potatoes (such as russet or good old brushed potatoes), peeled and cut into 2 cm cubes
200 g canned chopped tomatoes
2 golden shallots, peeled and quartered
3–4 garlic cloves, skin on, bashed with the back of a knife
150 ml dry white wine
2 tablespoons capers, rinsed and drained
2–3 tablespoons pitted black olives, roughly chopped
salt flakes and freshly ground black pepper
a few long red chillies, halved lengthways
3–4 tablespoons extra-virgin olive oil
basil leaves, to serve

SERVES 4

Preheat your oven to 200°C.

Place all the ingredients except the basil leaves in a baking dish and mix well.

Bake for 40 minutes or until the potato is cooked through and the tomato is nicely scorched. Top with basil leaves and enjoy!

Pan-roasted radicchio with crispy pancetta AND ALMONDS

Give me a bitter vegetable and I am one happy lady! I love them all, from endive to escarole, but my loyalties lie with the scarlet radicchio family: chioggia (the round one) and treviso (the oval one) steal my heart every time. They are delicious raw, but their sturdy leaves and core can handle a little heat as well, making them perfect for grilling. Treviso is often my first choice for this side dish, but chioggia works just as well, cut into wedges.

1 head of treviso radicchio,
   washed and well dried
80 ml (⅓ cup) olive oil
150 g pancetta, cut into
   small cubes
3 tablespoons balsamic vinegar
salt flakes and freshly ground
   black pepper
3–4 tablespoons almond flakes

SERVES 4

Trim the end of the radicchio and pull away and discard any damaged leaves. Cut the radicchio in half lengthways and score the root end.

Pour the olive oil into a large frying pan (big enough to fit the radicchio halves in one layer), add the pancetta and cook over medium–low heat for 3–4 minutes or until the pancetta is crispy and the fat has rendered out. Lift out the cooked pancetta with a slotted spoon and set aside.

Place the radicchio halves, cut-side down, in the pan and sizzle for 2 minutes on each side. Add the vinegar and 100 ml of water, then cover and cook for 8–10 minutes to soften the radicchio stem and wilt the leaves. Season with salt and pepper.

Meanwhile, toast the almond flakes in a separate frying pan over medium heat, shaking the pan for 1 minute or so until they start to smell fragrant and turn golden. Tip them onto a plate (if you leave them in the pan to cool, the residual heat will keep toasting them, and they might burn).

Place the cooked radicchio and juices on a serving plate, sprinkle with the pancetta and almonds and serve.

Nonna Carla's OVEN-BAKED fennel

Technically speaking, Nonna Carla was my cousin's grandmother – my uncle's mum, not a blood relation to me – but I would just call her Nonna for the ease of it and we established a very loving rapport, regardless of our lack of shared DNA. She would come to all my first concerts when I was a young opera singer in training (and possibly still rather pitchy!) and at family gatherings we would spend hours exchanging thoughts on Maria Callas and Big Luciano. Very much like my two grandmas she was also a great cook and, along with a passion for Verdi and Mozart, she passed on her recipe for oven-baked fennel, which she would cook in butter and milk, a testament to her northern Italian heritage. Just like art, family recipes are a treasure forever.

4 fennel bulbs (about 350 g each), trimmed and cut into 5 mm thick slices, fronds reserved
500 ml (2 cups) milk
¼ teaspoon freshly grated nutmeg
a few thyme sprigs
50 g (½ cup) freshly grated parmigiano
salt flakes and freshly ground black pepper
2 garlic cloves, skin on, bashed with the back of a knife
30 g butter, cut into cubes
3 tablespoons extra-virgin olive oil

SERVES 4

Preheat your oven to 200°C.

Place the fennel slices in a large baking dish. Add the milk, nutmeg, thyme and parmigiano, and season with salt and pepper. Top with the garlic, butter and olive oil.

Bake for 30–35 minutes or until the fennel is soft and the top is golden. Season with salt and pepper, scatter over the reserved fennel fronds and serve immediately.

Balsamic ROAST potatoes

Every Italian family has a tried-and-true recipe for roast potatoes, and whether it favours adding rosemary instead of thyme, leaving the garlic out or adding quartered shallots, the one common thread is that we roast them in extra-virgin olive oil, for maximum crunch and exceptional flavour. I also have a soft spot for a little sweet-and-sour note, and on special occasions I elevate my roast potato game by adding a touch of balsamic vinegar, both before and after baking, when the potatoes are hot and ready to take on more aromatics.

800 g red (russet or desiree) potatoes, skin on, each cut into 3–4 chunks
1 head of garlic, halved horizontally
3 tablespoons extra-virgin olive oil
3–4 tablespoons balsamic vinegar
salt flakes and freshly ground black pepper
thyme sprigs, to serve

SERVES 4

Preheat your oven to 200°C and line a baking tray with baking paper.

Place the potato in a saucepan of salted boiling water and cook for 15 minutes. Drain well.

Cut the potato into smaller chunks, keeping the skin intact. Place in a bowl with the garlic halves, olive oil, 2–3 tablespoons of the balsamic vinegar and salt and pepper, then toss together well. Transfer to the prepared tray and spread out in a single layer, placing the garlic halves cut-side down.

Roast for 30–35 minutes, then remove from the oven and gently toss the potato mixture, making sure they are still in a single layer. Turn the garlic halves over, then return to the oven for another 15–20 minutes or until the potato chunks are crunchy and dark golden and the garlic cloves are soft.

Once out of the oven, drizzle over the remaining balsamic vinegar, sprinkle with the thyme and serve.

NOTE
I add the thyme sprigs at the end so the aromas are released as they come into contact with the hot potatoes, but they don't dry out and become woody and unpalatable.

Green bean AND potato SALAD

This unassuming salad has been a family favourite ever since I can remember and is known amongst the Collocas as 'fagiolini e patate'. There are no fancy ingredients, just olive oil, herbs and a little garlic, so it is important to let the bold bareness of this dish shine. Mamma's trick is to cook the potatoes in a small pan (it needs to be quite a tight fit) of cold water seasoned with plenty of rock salt to ensure the potatoes retain their flavour and texture, without absorbing any moisture. The green beans are added at the very end, giving them just enough time to soften and bring out their natural sweetness.

800 g russet potatoes, skin on
2 handfuls of rock salt
400 g green beans, trimmed
    and cut into thirds
3–4 tablespoons extra-virgin
    olive oil
1 garlic clove, crushed
2 tablespoons white wine
    vinegar
salt flakes and freshly ground
    black or white pepper
baby basil and mint leaves,
    to serve

SERVES 4

Place the potatoes in a small saucepan so that they fit snugly. Cover with cold water, add the rock salt and bring to the boil. Reduce the heat to medium–low and simmer for 30–35 minutes or until the potatoes are almost cooked through.

Add the green beans and cook for 1–2 minutes. Drain both the beans and potatoes and allow to cool for 10 minutes.

Drizzle half the olive oil into a large mixing bowl and add the garlic. Peel the potatoes while they are still warm (the skin will come off more easily) and cut them into rough pieces, any size you like. Place them in the bowl, add the beans and toss them in the garlic oil. Add the vinegar and toss well, then taste for salt and adjust if necessary.

Tumble into a serving dish, drizzle with the remaining oil and dust with pepper. Top with a handful of baby basil and mint leaves and serve.

No more boring SOUPS—start BY CALLING THEM ZUPPA!

Soups play a huge role in an Italian household. Most families enjoy them nearly every night during the colder months, bulked up with legumes, bitter greens and sometimes grains or baby pasta. To be perfectly honest, I hardly need the memory of winter chills to crave a bowl of nourishing goodness – I am perfectly happy to enjoy it any time, rain or shine!

My younger children Miro and Luna are also strong believers in the soothing power of soup. It gets a little trickier with my husband Richard and our teenage son Raphael, who instinctively frown at the very idea of a 'liquid dinner', claiming soups are 'boring'.

How do we go about saving the reputation of such a humble preparation? Let's start by calling them zuppa! This might make you laugh, but if I answer the daily question of 'what's for dinner?' with a laconic 'soup', I am met with looks of disappointment, even a hint of despair. But if I announce 'tonight we are having zuppa!' the mood immediately lifts, as if the Italian word grants the wish of a richer, heartier meal.

In Italy, zuppa refers to a specific type of soup, dense and thick, and cooked with flavour boosters such as cheese rinds and pancetta. Light brothy soups go by the name of 'minestra' and are often enriched with greens and baby pasta or grains. We have a special name for baby pasta (and sometimes tortellini) cooked in broth – pastina – but don't be fooled by its unassuming appearance. It can be mighty filling, especially if cooked in a rich bone broth, the kind that my mamma makes on special occasions, and that I have permission to share with you.

NO MORE boring SOUPS – start BY CALLING THEM ZUPPA!

Quadrucci in BRODO (Fresh pasta squares IN broth)

For most Italian families, fresh pasta making is a favourite Sunday activity. And while the fruits of such labour are usually enjoyed at lunch, Sunday supper is what I look forward to when fresh pasta has been made. That is when the odd bits and pieces are cut into small squares and quickly cooked 'in brodo' (in a broth), which may be a simple chicken or vegetable one, or a collagen-rich, immune-boosting bone concoction. These go by a few different names in Italian households, such as brodino, pastina or minestrina, and all instantly conjure up a warming sense of comfort and safety.

I'm delighted to share my mamma's mighty good bone broth recipe, which is wonderful in this dish and for any meal requiring a restorative stock. As always, Mamma's recipes come with a set of rules:

1. Brown the meat and vegetables first, then add cold water to the pan and slowly bring to a simmer.
2. Don't let your stock boil ferociously. A gentle simmer is best and will prevent your stock from turning cloudy. Stirring the stock too much will also turn it cloudy.
3. Skim off the foam that comes to the surface in the first hour of simmering.
4. Make more than you need as it freezes well for up to 3 months.

If you have a pressure cooker, you might like to take it out of storage. It's fast and exceptionally effective for infusing bags of flavour into the liquid, ensuring all those precious aromas are trapped in a sealed environment.

You'll need to start this recipe a day ahead if you are making Mamma's broth from scratch.

When you are making fresh egg pasta (see page 20), reserve 250 g of the rolled sheets and cut them into small squares. It is important to do this while the pasta is still soft and hasn't dried out, otherwise it will be impossible to cut into neat squares. If you forget and the sheets dry out, don't despair – simply tear them into small uneven pieces for a dish brimming with rustic charm!

2 litres Mamma's Broth (see below)
or good-quality chicken or
vegetable stock
250 g leftover fresh pasta
sheets, cut into 2 cm squares
(see recipe intro)
freshly grated parmigiano,
to serve (optional)
salt flakes and freshly ground
black pepper

MAMMA'S BROTH

800 g mixed beef soup meat
(such as short ribs, shanks,
oxtail, bones and marrow – ask
your butcher for a selection)
6 chicken wings
2 onions, one roughly chopped,
one peeled and studded with
8 cloves
1 celery stalk, cut into 3 pieces
1 carrot, cut into 3 pieces
2 tablespoons extra-virgin
olive oil
salt flakes
2 bay leaves
1 star anise

SERVES 4

Preheat your oven to 220°C.

To make the broth, combine the meat, chicken wings, chopped onion, celery, carrot, olive oil and a pinch of salt in a large roasting tin and toss to combine. Roast for 30–40 minutes or until browned and slightly caramelised. Take out of the oven and, while still hot, pour in 500 ml (2 cups) of water and stir well to scrape up any bits caught on the base. Transfer everything to a large stockpot and pour in enough cold water to fully submerge everything. Add the bay leaves, star anise, clove-studded onion and 2–3 teaspoons of salt and slowly bring to a simmer. Cook gently over medium low heat for a minimum of 5 hours, skimming off the foam that comes to the surface during the first hour of cooking.

After the broth has had enough time, taste for salt and adjust if needed. Remove from the heat and let it cool completely at room temperature, then cover and place in the fridge for at least 6 hours or overnight. The fat will rise to the surface and set. The next day, scrape off the fat with a spoon and discard it. Strain the broth through a sieve. This makes enough broth for eight people, so freeze half and save it for another use.

Pour 2 litres of Mamma's broth or stock into a medium saucepan and bring to a simmer over medium heat. Drop in the pasta, stir and cook for 2 minutes or until cooked through but still retaining some texture.

Ladle into bowls, sprinkle with parmigiano, if you like, and season to taste with salt and pepper. Enjoy piping hot!

ZUPPA with chickpeas AND vongole

The marriage of seafood and legumes is one that Italians love to celebrate. Think braised cannellini beans with slow-cooked octopus or spaghetti with mussels and borlotti beans. Here I offer the heavenly union of creamy chickpeas and salty vongole, where each ingredient contributes to a wonderfully nourishing and complex flavour profile. This elegant zuppa is also gluten and dairy free.

3 tablespoons extra-virgin olive oil, plus extra for drizzling
1 small onion, finely chopped
1 carrot, finely chopped
1 celery stalk, finely chopped
2 tablespoons chopped flat-leaf parsley leaves
1 garlic clove, finely chopped
2 x 400 g cans chickpeas, drained and rinsed
1.5 litres good-quality vegetable stock
600 g vongole (clams), rinsed
salt flakes and freshly ground black pepper
2 rosemary sprigs, leaves picked and chopped

SERVES 4

Heat the olive oil in a large heavy-based saucepan over medium–high heat, add the onion, carrot, celery and parsley and cook for 1–2 minutes until slightly softened. Add the garlic and cook for another minute or until fragrant. Stir through the chickpeas and stock, then reduce the heat to low and simmer for 8–10 minutes until the liquid has reduced slightly.

Remove the pan from the heat and cool slightly. Transfer to a blender (or use a stick blender) and whiz until smooth, adding a little water if necessary to loosen.

Pour the soup back into the pan and bring to a simmer over medium heat. Add the vongole, then cover and cook, shaking the pan occasionally, for 2–3 minutes until the shells have opened (discard any that don't open). Season to taste with salt and pepper.

Ladle the soup into bowls and garnish with rosemary leaves and a good grinding of pepper. Drizzle with a little extra olive oil and serve.

LENTIL 'detox' minestrone

If the concept of a detox featuring Italian cuisine sounds like an oxymoron, let me introduce you to my vegan, gluten-free minestrone with a spring vibe: a healthy concoction of greens, fragrant herbs, legumes and olive oil, brimming with vitamins and nutrients, all mixed together in a recipe that can be adjusted to suit what you have in your fridge or pantry.

3 tablespoons extra-virgin olive oil, plus extra for drizzling
1 leek, well washed and thinly sliced
1 carrot, thinly sliced
1 celery stalk, thinly sliced
1 long red chilli, thinly sliced
1 garlic clove, finely chopped
200 g (1 cup) puy lentils
400 g can crushed tomatoes
2 potatoes, peeled and cut into small cubes
125 g green beans, trimmed and chopped
a few asparagus spears, woody ends removed, stems cut into 1 cm lengths, tips intact
100 g (⅔ cup) frozen peas
salt flakes and freshly ground black pepper
finely grated zest of 1 lemon
baby mint or basil leaves, to serve

SERVES 4

Heat the olive oil in a large heavy-based saucepan over medium heat. Add the leek, carrot, celery and chilli and cook for 2–3 minutes or until softened. Add the garlic and cook for another minute or until lightly golden.

Add the lentils, tomatoes and 2 litres of water. Bring to the boil, then reduce the heat to low and simmer for 15 minutes. Add the potato and cook for another 15 minutes. Stir in the beans, asparagus and peas and cook for 2–3 minutes until the lentils are nicely al dente and the potato is cooked through.

Season with salt and pepper and ladle into bowls. Drizzle with extra olive oil, top with the lemon zest and mint or basil leaves, and serve.

Pea AND crispy PANCETTA ZUPPA

This vibrant green zuppa ticks all the boxes when it comes to nutritional value, taste and looks. It's even gluten free! I've also included a great idea to make sure the potato skins are not wasted – bake them until crispy and completely irresistible, then serve them on the side with the pancetta for a double hit of salty crunch.

2 tablespoons extra-virgin olive oil, plus extra for drizzling
2 small onions, roughly chopped
2 garlic cloves, peeled and bashed with the palm of your hand
½ celery stalk, roughly chopped
2 potatoes, peeled and roughly chopped, peels reserved (see note)
a few thyme sprigs
piece of parmigiano rind (optional)
500 g (3⅓ cups) frozen peas
salt flakes and freshly ground black pepper
8 thin slices of pancetta
thyme leaves, to serve (optional)
pea tendrils, to serve (optional)

SERVES 4

Preheat your oven to 200°C and line a baking tray with baking paper.

Heat the olive oil in a large saucepan over medium heat, add the onion, garlic, celery, potato and thyme sprigs and cook for 3–4 minutes or until softened. Add the parmigiano rind (if using) and enough water to cover. Bring to a simmer, then reduce the heat to low and cook for 20 minutes or until all the veggies are soft. Add the peas and cook for a further 5 minutes. Remove the rind, then puree using a stick blender. Season to taste with salt and pepper.

While the soup is cooking, arrange the pancetta slices on the prepared tray and bake for 20–25 minutes or until crispy.

Ladle the soup into bowls and top with a grinding of pepper and some thyme and pea tendrils, if desired. Serve hot with the pancetta slices.

NOTE
If you like, you can roast the reserved potato peels to serve alongside this soup. Simply toss the peels with a little extra olive oil and salt and spread out on a baking tray lined with baking paper. Place in the oven at the same time as the pancetta and cook for 25–30 minutes or until golden and crispy.

Lentil AND pumpkin ZUPPA

Whoever said that Sydney doesn't really have a winter is a big liar! I've lived through my fair share since moving to Australia in 2009, and I can assure you the temperatures do drop, especially early in the morning and at night, when our dog Mabel is desperate for a run! Luckily, I have an array of weather-appropriate recipes like this delicious zuppa of pumpkin and lentil to instantly warm me up. Wherever you're spending your winter, I urge you to try this soup next time you're feeling the cold.

3 tablespoons extra-virgin olive oil
3 golden shallots or 1 onion, chopped
400 g pumpkin (butternut or kent), peeled, deseeded and chopped
50 g piece of smoked pancetta or speck (ham hock or even chorizo would also work)
200 g (1 cup) puy lentils
500 ml (2 cups) good-quality vegetable stock
8 cavolo nero or kale leaves, stalks removed, chopped

TO SERVE
flat-leaf parsley leaves
finely grated lemon zest
chopped red chilli
chilli oil (optional)

SERVES 4

Heat the olive oil in a large saucepan over medium heat. Add the shallot or onion and cook for 2–3 minutes until softened. Add the pumpkin and pancetta or speck and cook for a few minutes until lightly coloured.

Add the lentils, stock and enough water to cover everything, then reduce the heat to medium–low and simmer for 35–40 minutes or until the pumpkin is soft and the lentils are al dente.

Discard the pancetta, then add the cavolo nero or kale and stir through. Remove from the heat and allow it to wilt in the residual heat.

Ladle into bowls and finish with parsley leaves, lemon zest, red chilli and chilli oil, if desired. Any combination will be delicious.

Minestra di pasta mista WITH potatoes AND CHICKPEAS

My mamma kept this soup on high rotation when we were growing up, not only because it's delicious and nutritious, but also because it's cooked in one pot: no straining, no mess, no extra washing up. And it's the perfect way to use up nearly-empty packets of pasta. Of course, it makes sense to pair shapes with a similar cooking time, but if you have different shapes just add them in descending order of cooking time. If the concept of carb on carb seems a bit much, just humour me and try it – you'll be amazed by how well pasta and potatoes go together. The potatoes almost dissolve into the broth, creating a luscious coating for perfectly al dente pasta. It's the stuff of dreams!

Because it includes pasta, this soup is referred to as a minestra rather than a zuppa (see page 214), and it can be made thinner or thicker, depending on how much water you cook it in. My preference is for it to be just slightly wet, and covering the ingredients with about 8 cm of water will give you just that.

3 tablespoons extra-virgin olive oil, plus extra to serve
1 golden shallot, finely chopped
1 small celery stalk, thinly sliced, leaves reserved
80 g piece of pancetta, cut into thin strips
400 g potato, peeled and cut into small cubes
1 small parmigiano or pecorino rind
400 g can chickpeas, drained and rinsed
salt flakes and freshly ground black pepper
200 g canned chopped tomatoes
320 g pasta mista (leftover mixed pasta)
freshly grated parmigiano or pecorino, to serve
crusty bread, to serve

SERVES 4

Fill your kettle with water and put it on to boil.

Heat the olive oil in a saucepan over medium heat, add the shallot, celery and pancetta and cook for 2–3 minutes until the pancetta starts to brown and the onion is translucent. Add the potato, cheese rind, chickpeas and enough boiling water to just cover and season with salt and pepper. Cook for 5–6 minutes or until the potato has softened.

Add the tomatoes, pasta and enough boiling water to cover everything by 8 cm. Stir gently and cook for 8–9 minutes or until the pasta is al dente.

Discard the cheese rind, then ladle into bowls. Finish with freshly ground pepper, a little extra olive oil, grated cheese and the reserved celery leaves, if you like. Serve hot with some crusty bread.

Onion AND almond ZUPPA

If you like French onion soup, you'll love its southern Italian cousin, which celebrates ingredients traditionally grown in Calabria, such as almonds and sweet red Tropea onions, all brought together with piquant extra-virgin olive oil and a pinch of cinnamon. All you need is crusty bread and a nice glass of red!

By the way, regular red onions will also work well here. I'm assuming Tropea onions are hard to come by when you're 13,000 kilometres away from Calabria.

3 tablespoons extra-virgin olive oil
20 g unsalted butter
5 red onions, thinly sliced
1 garlic clove, finely chopped
1.5 litres good-quality beef stock
100 g (⅔ cup) blanched almonds, chopped
1 tablespoon white wine vinegar
2 teaspoons raw sugar
salt flakes and freshly ground black pepper
1 teaspoon ground cinnamon
3 thyme sprigs, leaves picked, plus extra leaves to serve
3 tablespoons freshly grated pecorino
crusty bread, to serve (optional)

SERVES 4

Heat the olive oil and butter in a large saucepan over medium–low heat, add the onion and garlic and cook, stirring occasionally, for 20–25 minutes until caramelised.

Pour in 500 ml (2 cups) of the stock and bring to a simmer. Reduce the heat to low and cook, covered, for 20–25 minutes until slightly reduced. Add the almonds, vinegar and sugar and stir to combine. Pour in the remaining stock and simmer for a further 25–30 minutes until the onion is beautifully soft and the liquid has reduced a little. Season to taste with salt and pepper.

Preheat the grill function on your oven to medium–high.

Ladle the soup into four ovenproof bowls. Sprinkle with the cinnamon and scatter over the thyme and pecorino. Place the bowls under the grill and cook for 2 minutes or until the cheese has melted.

Scatter over some extra thyme leaves and finish with a good grinding of pepper. Serve hot with some crusty bread, if you like.

Classic winter MINESTRONE

Minestrone is the epitome of Italian zuppa and the ultimate winter warmer. How can you go wrong when your meal is packed with robust dark green leaves, antioxidants and vitamins? Add the nutrients of borlotti beans and extra-virgin olive oil, plus the kick of chilli, and you have yourself a spa treatment for your insides that is sure to keep you warm and satisfied. Minestrone is much more than just a soup; it's so rich and healthy that you'll feel revitalised with every mouthful.

3 tablespoons extra-virgin olive oil, plus extra to serve
1 leek, well washed and thinly sliced
1 garlic clove, finely chopped
1 small carrot, sliced
1 celery stalk, sliced
1 small parmigiano rind (optional)
small handful of diced pancetta or speck (optional)
2 potatoes, chopped
160 g (⅔ cup) canned chopped tomatoes
400 g can borlotti beans, drained and rinsed
salt flakes and freshly ground black pepper
8–10 brussels sprouts, outer leaves removed, quartered
4–5 cavolo nero leaves, stalks removed, shredded
135 g (¾ cup) baby pasta (such as anellini, ditalini or orzo)
chilli oil, to serve (optional)

SERVES 4

Heat the olive oil in a large heavy-based saucepan over medium heat. Add the leek, garlic, carrot and celery and cook for 2–3 minutes or until softened. Add the parmigiano rind and pancetta or speck (if using).

Add the potato and tomatoes and cover with water. Bring to the boil, then reduce the heat to low and simmer for 25 minutes. Add the borlotti beans and cook for another 20 minutes or until the potato and beans are tender. Season with salt and pepper (only salt the beans once they're cooked or they will wrinkle up).

Stir in the brussels sprouts, cavolo nero and baby pasta and cook for 7–8 minutes or until the pasta is nicely al dente. Remove from the heat.

Discard the parmigiano rind, if using, and ladle the soup into bowls. Finish with a good swirl of extra olive oil or chilli oil.

NOTES
Omit the parmigiano rind and pancetta or speck for a vegan soup.

Use arborio rice instead of pasta for a gluten-free version.

Virtuous PANE RAFFERMO (leftover BREAD)

It is only fitting that a population so profoundly devoted to bread would boast an extensive collection of recipes for when it's past its prime. In the following pages, you will discover some ingenious ideas to make the most of stale bread, a small but representative selection of our family classics.

I am confident that if I put my mind to it I could dedicate an entire book to leftover bread recipes, and maybe one day I will! For now, I will leave you with my absolute favourites, hoping they will inspire you to breathe new life into stale bread and turn it into something spectacular.

Virtuous PANE raffermo (leftover BREAD)

Leftover BREAD gnocchetti AND chickpeas

Most Italian home cooks have a treasured recipe for pasta e ceci (chickpeas) up their sleeve. It's one of those virtuous dishes that ticks all the boxes when it comes to flavour, nutritional value and resourcefulness. I was lucky enough to inherit both Abruzzese and Piacentina recipes.

My great aunt Maria's pasta e ceci gained legendary status in my family when, during a visit to her house in the Colli Piacentini, she presented my siblings and me with a bowl of her signature dish, gnocchetti di pane e ceci. Up until that day, pesky children that we were, we would turn up our noses at the mere sight of a chickpea, but one quick but effective 'evil' look from Mamma and Papà made it clear that we were not to offend our old Zia so we reluctantly dug in. And then went back for more, and more, until there was none left in the pot. This was a massive win for my parents, and the beginning of my life-long passion for the humble chickpea.

350 g dried chickpeas
1 celery stalk
1 onion, whole and skin on
salt flakes and freshly ground
    black pepper
2½ tablespoons extra-virgin
    olive oil, plus extra to serve
2 garlic cloves, skin on, bashed
    with the back of a knife
30 g piece of pancetta or speck
1 teaspoon finely chopped
    rosemary leaves
250 g canned chopped
    tomatoes
1 small parmigiano or
    pecorino rind
freshly grated parmigiano,
    to serve (optional)

GNOCCHETTI
400 g (2⅔ cups) plain flour,
    plus extra for dusting
30 g fresh breadcrumbs
pinch of salt flakes
200 ml hot water, plus extra
    if needed

SERVES 4

Soak the chickpeas in a large bowl of water overnight. The next day, drain then place them in a large saucepan and cover with water. Add the celery and onion and bring to a simmer over medium–high heat. Reduce the heat to low and cook for 1–1½ hours until tender. Once the chickpeas are cooked, season with salt and pepper, then leave to cool completely in the poaching liquid. Once cool, drain and discard the celery and onion.

Heat the olive oil in a large heavy-based frying pan or flameproof casserole dish over high heat, add the garlic, pancetta or speck and rosemary and cook for a few minutes, then add the chickpeas, tomatoes, cheese rind and enough water to cover everything by 5 cm. Reduce the heat to low and simmer for 30–45 minutes. Taste and season with salt and pepper if needed. Remove and discard the garlic cloves, cheese rind and pancetta or speck.

Meanwhile, to make the gnocchetti, place the flour, breadcrumbs and salt in a bowl, make a well in the centre and pour in enough hot water to form a dough similar to pasta dough. Knead for 10 minutes or until smooth and elastic, then wrap in plastic wrap or a beeswax wrap and set aside to rest at room temperature for 30 minutes.

Cut the dough into six or seven pieces. Roll each piece into a 2 cm thick sausage, then cut into 2 cm lengths. Using your thumb, create an indent in the middle of each piece, then dust with flour and set aside.

Cook the gnocchetti in a large saucepan of salted boiling water for 3–4 minutes or until they float to the surface (very much like gnocchi). Fish them out with a slotted spoon and drop them straight into the chickpea sauce. Add a little of the cooking water to loosen the sauce to a soupy consistency. Gently toss, then rest for a few minutes to allow the flavours to mingle. Drizzle with a little extra olive oil, top with some parmigiano (if desired) and enjoy!

Pappa col POMODORO (Summer bread and tomato SOUP)

You'll always find this Tuscan classic on Italian tables at the end of summer when tomatoes are at their ripest. The main ingredient, however, is stale bread, left to simmer in tomato juices, stock and olive oil until it turns into a thick soup. This is a truly magical dish where a few humble ingredients create the loveliest, freshest meal of the season, which also happens to be vegan.

So what are you waiting for? Seek out full-bodied extra-virgin olive oil and the juiciest tomatoes you can find and turn your stale bread into your new favourite summer dish. Don't even think of making it any other time of the year...

1 kg roma or vine-ripened
  tomatoes
iced water, for refreshing
3 tablespoons extra-virgin olive
  oil, plus extra for drizzling
1 small onion, finely chopped
salt flakes and freshly ground
  black pepper
2 garlic cloves, finely chopped
250 g crustless day-old
  sourdough bread, cut
  into chunks
good-quality vegetable stock,
  to cover
basil leaves, to serve

SERVES 4

Score the tomatoes, then plunge them into a large saucepan of simmering water for 1 minute. Drain and place them in a bowl of iced water. You will now be able to easily pinch off the skins. Roughly chop the peeled tomatoes and set aside.

Heat the olive oil in a large heavy-based saucepan over medium heat, add the onion and a pinch of salt and cook for a few minutes until softened and slightly coloured. Add the garlic and cook for 1 minute, keeping an eye on it as it can burn easily. Drop in the tomato, season with a bit more salt and mix through. Add the bread, then pour in enough stock to completely cover everything. Bring to a simmer, then reduce the heat to low and cook, covered, for 45–60 minutes or until the bread has surrendered and the soup has a custard-like consistency. Check occasionally as it cooks and add a splash more stock or water if it starts to dry out.

Ladle the soup into bowls and finish with a grinding of pepper, a good drizzle of olive oil and a scattering of basil leaves. Enjoy hot, warm or at room temperature.

Mozza-rella in carrozza (FRIED MOZZARELLA toastie)

Mozzarella in carrozza literally means 'mozzarella in a horse-drawn carriage' and I can't for the life of me understand why a fried sandwich would be named after this vehicle. As a child I used to pretend the sandwich was the carriage itself and I would make it trot in the air, pulled by imaginary horses. Maybe the name was given to stimulate the innate creativity of children. Perhaps simply calling this humble preparation 'stale bread fried mozzarella toastie' would not have inspired child's play!

8 slices of stale sandwich bread, crusts removed
2 x 125 g mozzarella balls, well drained, sliced
olive oil, for shallow-frying
125 ml (½ cup) milk
3 heaped tablespoons plain flour
1 large egg
salt flakes and freshly ground black pepper

SERVES 4

Make four sandwiches out of the bread and mozzarella, leaving a little border around the edges. Press the edges with your fingers to seal.

Add enough olive oil to generously coat the base of a non-stick frying pan and place over medium heat.

Meanwhile, pour the milk into one shallow bowl, the flour into another, and beat the egg with salt and pepper in another.

Dunk the sandwiches in the milk, then dredge in the flour and dip in the beaten egg. Add to the pan in batches and cook for 2 minutes each side or until golden and crispy. Drain on paper towel, season with salt and pepper and serve hot.

Pan–zanella

Panzanella is another great example of how well Italians do when the fridge and pantry look a little bare. It's easy to create a stunning meal out of sophisticated ingredients, but it requires a lot more skill and creativity to prepare a delicious, nutritious dish out of stale bread and a handful of frugal staples.

Although the classic Tuscan version of panzanella features only tomatoes, cucumber, onion and vinegar, the recipe can be easily pimped up and turned into something special. As always, I do exercise caution when adding new ingredients to classic recipes; I like to think the disarming simplicity of this dish is perfect enough.

The Tuscans bathe the bread in their piquant extra-virgin olive oil, so robust it's almost peppery, and I would advise you to try and find an olive oil with a similar flavour, as it will really bring this dish to life.

A little disclaimer: the original recipe doesn't call for the bread to be toasted; the stale bread is simply soaked in water and vinegar until soft, then broken up into a pulp. While I love it the way it was first created, I do like a crunchy edge on my bread chunks, so here I give them a little time in the oven, then drizzle them lightly with vinegar, more like a seasoning than a bath. I hope my Tuscan relatives can forgive me (they will probably never know as they don't speak English anyway).

1 red onion, thinly sliced into rings (I use a mandoline)
80 ml (⅓ cup) aged red wine vinegar, plus extra to serve
salt flakes and freshly ground black pepper
250 g stale sourdough, cut into chunks
3 tablespoons extra-virgin olive oil, plus extra to serve
1 cucumber
4 large heirloom tomatoes, sliced and quartered
150 g cherry tomatoes, halved
basil leaves, to serve

SERVES 4

Preheat your oven to 200°C and line a baking tray with baking paper.

Place the onion and vinegar in a small bowl. Add enough water to cover the onion rings, then season with salt and pepper and toss to combine. Set aside to pickle for 20–30 minutes.

Place the sourdough and half the olive oil in a bowl, season and toss to coat. Spread out on the prepared tray and bake for 20–25 minutes or until crisp and golden. Remove and set aside.

Drain the onion, reserving 3–4 tablespoons of the pickling juices. Drizzle the liquid over the toasted bread and toss well.

Cut the cucumber in half lengthways, then scoop out the seeds and discard them, as they can be hard to digest. Finely chop the cucumber.

Place the bread chunks, tomatoes, cucumber, onion and the remaining olive oil in a bowl and toss together. Taste and season with salt and pepper if needed, and add a little more red wine vinegar if you like. Top with plenty of basil leaves and drizzle with a little extra olive oil.

GNUDI
with ricotta
AND SPINACH

Call them dumplings, gnudi or patties, these deliciously soft morsels will have you beaming with delight at the very first bite. What could go wrong when you combine the milky richness of fresh ricotta (always full cream!) with homemade breadcrumbs, zingy herbs and the warmth of nutmeg? These gnudi are poached in a fresh tomato sauce, ready to be devoured with a generous chunk of crusty bread or gently mixed through perfectly al dente spaghetti. Or enjoy them just as they are, like my dear friend Vitina is in the picture opposite!

semolina flour (see note page 38), for dusting

TOMATO SAUCE
850 g ripe tomatoes
iced water, for refreshing
3 tablespoons extra-virgin olive oil
2 golden shallots (or 1 onion), finely chopped
1 small celery stalk, finely chopped
1 garlic clove, skin on, bashed with the back of a knife
salt flakes, to taste
handful of basil leaves

GNUDI
1 tablespoon extra-virgin olive oil
1 garlic clove, bashed with the back of a knife
600 g baby spinach leaves
450 g fresh ricotta
1 egg
½ teaspoon salt flakes
pinch of ground white pepper
100 g (1¼ cups) fresh breadcrumbs (see note), plus extra if needed
50 g freshly grated pecorino, plus extra if needed
good handful of flat-leaf parsley leaves, chopped
½ teaspoon freshly grated nutmeg
2–3 tablespoons milk (optional)

SERVES 4

Start by making the tomato sauce. Score the tomatoes, then plunge them into a large saucepan of simmering water for 1 minute. Drain and place them in a bowl of iced water. You will now be able to easily pinch off the skins. Roughly chop the peeled tomatoes and set aside.

Heat the olive oil in a large heavy-based frying pan over medium heat. Add the shallot, celery and garlic and cook for 1–2 minutes or until the shallot is translucent and lightly golden. Add the tomato and 125 ml (½ cup) of water, season with salt, then reduce the heat to medium–low and simmer for 15–20 minutes. Remove from the heat and discard the garlic cloves. (For a smoother sauce, blitz in a food processor for 4–5 seconds.) Scatter some basil leaves on top, then cover and set aside.

While the sauce is simmering, make the gnudi. Heat the olive oil in a saucepan over high heat, add the garlic and spinach, then cover and allow to wilt for 2–3 minutes. Set aside to cool, then drain off the excess liquid, discard the garlic clove and roughly chop the spinach.

Place the spinach and remaining ingredients (except the milk) in a large bowl and mix well. It should feel sticky, but workable. If it's too dry, add a little milk; if it's too wet, add a little extra cheese or breadcrumbs. Cover and place in the fridge for 30 minutes or overnight to firm up.

Line a baking tray with baking paper and dust with semolina flour. Using wet hands, shape the gnudi mixture into balls the size of a golf ball, then place on the prepared tray until you're ready to cook.

Reheat the tomato sauce, adding a little water if it looks dry. When the sauce comes to a simmer, gently drop in the gnudi. Cover and let the steam cook them for 5–6 minutes. Remove the lid and, using a wooden spoon, gently turn them over. They are extremely delicate, so be careful! Cook uncovered for another minute, then remove from the heat.

You can eat the gnudi immediately, though I often serve them the next day when they are firmer and the flavours are more developed. Simply store them in the fridge overnight, then gently reheat before serving.

NOTE
To make your own breadcrumbs, simply place chunks of stale bread in a food processor and blitz to a coarse crumb.

Melanzane ripiene (Stuffed EGGPLANT)

Whether you call it eggplant, aubergine or melanzane, let's all agree that this spongy, tangy fruit is one of nature's great gifts. Its versatility is such that it can be deep-fried, grilled, charred or pan-fried. You can even use it to replace lasagne sheets (hello parmigiana!). But when eggplants are stuffed with ricotta and tomato, then topped with breadcrumbs and parmigiano, well, that's when I go weak at the knees! This vegetarian Sicilian-style dish is my go-to meal at the end of summer, when eggplants are in season.

3-4 small eggplants (or Japanese eggplants), halved lengthways
120 ml extra-virgin olive oil, plus extra for drizzling
salt flakes and freshly ground black pepper
1-2 garlic cloves, skin on, bashed with the back of a knife
400 ml Quick and Easy Passata (see page 29) or 400 g can chopped tomatoes
large handful of basil leaves, chopped
250 g fresh ricotta
60 g freshly grated parmigiano, plus extra for dusting
1 egg, lightly beaten
50 g stale sourdough, blitzed to coarse breadcrumbs
freshly grated ricotta salata or pecorino, to serve
flat-leaf parsley or basil leaves, to serve

SERVES 4

Preheat your oven to 200°C and line a large baking tray with baking paper.

Using a knife, carefully remove the flesh from the eggplant halves, being careful not to cut through the skin. You want to keep the skin intact so that you have empty eggplant boats ready to welcome the filling. Chop the eggplant flesh into 1 cm pieces and set aside.

Oil the eggplant shells with 1-2 tablespoons of the olive oil and season with a little salt and pepper. Place, cut-side up, on the prepared tray and bake for 30 minutes.

Meanwhile, heat the remaining olive oil in a frying pan over medium heat, add the eggplant pieces and garlic and cook for 4–5 minutes until they start to colour. Add the passata or tomatoes and most of the basil, season with salt and cook, stirring occasionally, for 20 minutes.

Make the filling by combining the ricotta, parmigiano, beaten egg and the remaining basil in a bowl. Season with salt and pepper, then add the eggplant and tomato sauce and mix well.

Spoon the filling into the eggplant shells. Top with the breadcrumbs, then dust with extra parmigiano. Drizzle with a little extra olive oil and bake for 20 minutes or until golden.

Grate some ricotta salata on top when they are fresh out of the oven. If you don't have ricotta salata, try some peppery pecorino. Sprinkle with some parsley or basil leaves and finish with a final drizzle of olive oil.

Canederli in BRODO (Leftover dumplings in BROTH)

This nourishing soup, typical of the south Tyrolean region on the border with Switzerland and Austria, is a great example of how diverse Italian cuisine is. Each dish is deeply connected to its territory and its unique traditions. Canederli are stale bread dumplings floating in a rich amber broth, a meal you would certainly crave after a day on the slopes in the Dolomites. And even though the Collocas were never known for their skiing expertise, Mamma would make this dish for us in winter, when Milan was shrouded in fog. The thought of this meal waiting for us when we got home from school somehow made the bitter cold more bearable.

20 g butter
1 tablespoon extra-virgin olive oil
1 small onion, finely chopped
150 g speck, cut into very small
   pieces (the smaller the better)
2–3 sage leaves, finely chopped
250 g stale bread, crusts
   removed
200 ml milk
2 eggs, lightly beaten
salt flakes and freshly ground
   black pepper
1 tablespoon chopped chives
30 g fresh breadcrumbs, plus
   extra if needed
2 litres good-quality chicken
   stock or Mamma's Broth
   (see page 217)
freshly grated parmigiano,
   to serve

SERVES 4

Heat the butter and olive oil in a frying pan over medium heat, add the onion, speck and sage and cook for 2 minutes or until the onion has softened. Set aside to cool.

Cut the bread into small cubes and place in a bowl. Add the milk and egg and mix well. Use your hands to squish the bread so that it absorbs the milk and egg.

Add the cooled onion mixture and stir through. Season with salt and pepper, then add the chives and just enough fresh breadcrumbs to bind the mixture together. Shape into dumplings the size of walnuts (keep in mind that they grow bigger when you poach them).

Pour the stock into a large saucepan and bring to a simmer. Gently drop in the canederli and cook over low heat, partially covered, for 12–15 minutes. When the canederli are cooked through, remove from the heat and ladle into bowls, along with the broth. Dust with parmigiano and serve hot.

Baked chicken WITH bread, cherry tomatoes, OLIVES AND capers

If you have never tried wedging chunks of stale bread in your roast chicken tray I hope this recipe will convince you to start, either with a whole chicken or pieces, as I have done here. The stale bread acts as a sponge, soaking up the tomato juices and chicken dripping as well as the beautiful olive oil and wine. In the process, the crumb becomes lusciously soft, while the edges become charred and crunchy, quickly turning the stale bread into the undisputed star of the dish.

250 g cherry tomatoes, halved
60 g (½ cup) pitted black olives
3 tablespoons capers (or to taste), rinsed and drained
125 ml (½ cup) dry white wine
100 ml extra-virgin olive oil
3 thick slices of stale sourdough, cut into chunks
thyme sprigs, for sprinkling, plus extra to serve
salt flakes and freshly ground black pepper
8 chicken thigh fillets, skin on

SERVES 4

Preheat your oven to 180°C.

Oil a roasting tin, then add the cherry tomatoes and their juices, olives, capers, wine and half the olive oil. Mix well, then scatter over the bread chunks and a little thyme and season with salt. Place the chicken on top, season with salt and pepper and spoon over some of the liquid in the base of the tin.

Bake for 40–45 minutes or until the chicken is cooked through and the skin is crisp and golden. The cooking time will depend on the size of your chicken pieces, so keep an eye on them.

Take the tin out of the oven. Spoon some of the delicious sauce over the chicken, scatter more thyme sprigs on top and serve.

Classic polpette (MEATBALLS)

How many of you recall that famous scene from Disney's *Lady and the Tramp*, when the love-struck dogs share a long spaghetto strand? In a memorable gesture, Tramp nudges the last meatball over to Lady, as a symbol of his love and devotion. He's a keeper, Lady!

While the classic Italian iconography portrays giant bowls of spaghetti mingling with round polpette, we generally eat the two separately. We dress the pasta with the rich sauce the meatballs have been simmering in, and savour the delightful nuggets another day, served simply with chunky bread or soft polenta. Cook once, eat twice: a motto all Italian home cooks live by!

2 thick slices of stale bread, crusts removed, cut into chunks
250 ml (1 cup) milk
450 g veal and pork mince
1 egg
handful of flat-leaf parsley leaves, chopped
¼ teaspoon freshly grated nutmeg
35 g (⅓ cup) freshly grated parmigiano
salt flakes and freshly ground white pepper
3 tablespoons extra-virgin olive oil
1 onion, chopped
1 garlic clove, skin on, bashed with the back of a knife
125 ml (½ cup) red wine
1 bay leaf
2 x 400 g cans chopped tomatoes
spaghetti, crusty bread or soft polenta, to serve

SERVES 4

Soak the bread in the milk for about 10 minutes.

Place the mince, egg, parsley, nutmeg, parmigiano, 2 teaspoons of salt and 1 teaspoon of white pepper in a bowl and mix well. Use a spoon if you feel squeamish about touching raw meat, but in my opinion hands are your best kitchen tool.

Squeeze the milk out of the bread, then mix the soft bread into the mince mixture.

Roll the mixture into balls the size of small mandarins. Place on a tray and chill in the fridge for 15 minutes to firm up.

Meanwhile, heat the olive oil in a large frying pan over medium heat, add the onion and garlic and cook for a few minutes until the onion is soft and translucent.

Add the meatballs and brown on all sides. Deglaze the pan with the wine, scraping up any bits caught on the base, and simmer until the alcohol has evaporated (this should take about 2 minutes).

Add the bay leaf, tomatoes and 250 ml (1 cup) of water. Bring to the boil, then reduce the heat to low and simmer, covered, for at least 2 hours, stirring occasionally. Taste and season with salt and pepper if needed. Serve the meatballs just as they are or with spaghetti, crusty bread or soft polenta. They're also delicious with your favourite greens.

SWEET AND SIMPLE

Italians are well known for having a sweet tooth; after all, we created delights such as tiramisu, biscotti and panettone! However, one fundamental truth about our sugar intake is that we prefer it unadorned – you won't find elaborately decorated layered cakes or unicorn-shaped ombre macarons in an Italian pasticceria (pastry shop). We do like it sweet, but we like it even more if it's simple. And the recipes featured in this chapter perfectly embody this sentiment.

It goes to show that if your kitchen is well stocked with essentials, such as flour, eggs and sugar, you can easily satisfy sweet cravings on a whim. Some of the recipes included here don't even require any actual baking, nor instruments of precision. As always, it's all about simplicity and common sense, mixed with a little bit of chemistry!

SWEET AND SIMPLE

JAM
bomboloni

In Italy we have our very own type of doughnut, but, unlike its Anglo-Saxon cousin, the bomboloni remains in one piece without a big hole in the middle. You see, we Italians need that belly of dough to hold a tasty filling, like jam or custard, ready to gush out at the first bite!

7 g sachet dried yeast
120 ml milk, slightly warmed
   (to body temperature)
3 tablespoons caster sugar,
   plus extra for coating
250 g (1⅔ cups) plain flour,
   plus extra for dusting
2 eggs, beaten
50 g butter, melted
pinch of salt flakes
finely grated zest of 1 lemon
vegetable oil, for deep-frying
your favourite jam, for filling

MAKES 6

Mix the yeast and milk in a large bowl. Add 1 teaspoon of the sugar and stand for a few minutes to froth up.

Add the flour, egg, butter, salt, lemon zest and the remaining sugar to the yeast mixture and mix to form a rough dough. If you have a stand mixer fitted with a dough hook, knead it on medium speed for 5 minutes or until the dough is smooth and elastic. Otherwise, just tip the rough dough onto a floured board or bench and knead for up to 10 minutes or until smooth.

Place the dough in a bowl, dust it lightly with flour and cover with a damp tea towel. Leave at room temperature for 2–3 hours or until the dough has more than doubled in size. In very hot climates, try to find a cooler spot (not the fridge) or it will rise too quickly. In very cold temperatures it may take a little longer to rise.

When the dough has risen, turn it out onto a clean floured surface and roll it out to 2.5 cm thick. Cut out six rounds with a 5 cm cookie cutter or ramekin and place them on a sheet of baking paper. Cover and leave to rise again for 30–45 minutes, until risen by about two-thirds.

Pour a generous amount of extra sugar onto a plate.

Pour vegetable oil into a deep frying pan, making sure you have enough to fully submerge the bomboloni. Add the balls in two batches and cook for 2–3 minutes each side until they are golden and cooked through. Lift them out with a slotted spoon and drop them straight into the sugar, then roll to coat them all over. Add more sugar as needed.

Cool the bomboloni on a wire rack for 15–20 minutes, then pipe your favourite jam into the centre. These are best enjoyed on the day you make them.

Torta margherita (DAISY CAKE)

This gluten-free, dairy-free sponge cake was first created some two hundred years ago, back when the only dietary restrictions were the ones dictated by poverty. Italian home cooking is a well of such recipes, all showcasing the prudent nature of this timeless cuisine. Over the years, more lavish ingredients such as butter and flour have found their way into the batter, but I would love to share this cake with you in its original, humble incarnation, as a tribute to those who came before us and left this precious legacy.

Traditionally, torta margherita is served simply dusted with icing sugar; the white-topped slices look a little like daisy petals, hence the romantic name. If you feel inspired and have a knack for arts and crafts, create your own petal stencil and snow some icing sugar over it. Full disclosure though: the dainty pattern you see here is the work of my bestie Jono Fleming ... I think I'm too impatient for this careful symmetrical labour!

130 g caster sugar
4 eggs, separated
130 g potato starch, sifted
finely grated zest of 1 lemon
juice of ½ lemon
icing sugar, for dusting

SERVES 8–10

Preheat your oven to 180°C. Grease and line a 20 cm round cake tin with baking paper.

Place the sugar and egg yolks in a stand mixer fitted with a whisk attachment and whisk for 3–5 minutes or until fluffy and tripled in volume. You can do this by hand if you don't have a mixer; just be prepared to whisk for a good 10 minutes. Add the potato starch, lemon zest and lemon juice and beat in gently.

In a separate, clean bowl, beat the egg whites until soft peaks form, then very gently fold them into the yolk mixture. Pour the batter into the prepared tin, level the top with a spoon or spatula and bake for 50–55 minutes or until golden and set and a skewer inserted into the centre comes out clean.

Cool in the tin for 15 minutes, then turn out onto a wire rack to cool completely. Dust with plenty of icing sugar and serve. Leftovers will keep in an airtight container for up to 2 days.

PANFORTE

Panforte is as traditionally Italian as it gets. Legend has it that on the way to their quest, crusaders used to carry slabs of what was described as a durable confection made with honey, sugar syrup, spices, nuts and dried fruits. Its name means 'strong bread', which refers to the generous quantity of spices, such as clove and cinnamon, as well as black pepper. It is one of the most loved Italian confections and is usually consumed around Christmas, especially in Tuscany, its geographical homeland.

If you like, you can use a kitchen thermometer to make this. They are easy to buy in kitchenware shops or online. Or you can just use your eyes and instincts.

100 g (⅔ cup) whole blanched almonds
105 g (¾ cup) roasted hazelnuts, skins removed
100 g semi-dried figs, coarsely chopped
55 g (⅓ cup) mixed peel
150 g (1 cup) plain flour
2 tablespoons Dutch cocoa powder
2 teaspoons ground cinnamon
½ teaspoon ground cloves
¼ teaspoon freshly grated nutmeg
¼ teaspoon freshly ground black pepper
350 g (1 cup) honey, plus extra if needed
80 g dark chocolate, chopped
115 g (½ cup) caster sugar

SERVES 8–10

Preheat your oven to 170°C. Grease an 18–20 cm round cake tin and line with baking paper.

Place the almonds, hazelnuts, figs and peel in a large bowl.

Sift the flour, cocoa and spices into a separate bowl.

Combine the honey, chocolate and sugar in a saucepan over medium heat. Bring to the boil, then reduce the heat to low and simmer, without stirring, for 2 minutes or until bubbly and thickened and the mixture reaches 116°C on a kitchen thermometer. Remove from the heat, then add the dry ingredients and nut mixture and stir to form a dark, sticky paste (if the mixture doesn't come together, add an extra tablespoon of honey).

Using a spoon, press the mixture evenly into the prepared tin. Bake for 30–35 minutes until just set. Cool slightly, then turn out onto a wire rack to cool completely. Cut into slices and store in an airtight container at room temperature for up to 4 weeks.

Cherry AND ricotta CAKE

Cherry season has always held a special place in my heart. When I was a child, their presence at market stalls heralded the end of the school year and the beginning of the Italian summer, two of the things I held most dear! Alas, very much like summer holidays, cherry season comes and goes way too quickly and my only solution is to make the most of these ruby jewels while they are around. I eat them fresh, turn them into jam, preserve them in grappa (it's amazing!) and, of course, pit them and stir them into cake batters.

2 eggs
110 g brown sugar
finely grated zest of 1 lemon and 1 orange
1 vanilla bean, split and seeds scraped
2½ tablespoons olive oil
200 g firm fresh ricotta
200 g (1⅓ cups) self-raising flour
300 g pitted cherries
icing sugar, for dusting
extra cherries and whipped cream, to serve (optional)

SERVES 8–10

Preheat your oven to 180°C. Grease a 20 cm round cake tin and line with baking paper.

Whisk the eggs and sugar until pale and fluffy. Stir in the citrus zest, vanilla seeds and olive oil. Add the ricotta and gently beat in, then sift in the flour and stir gently until just combined. Fold in the cherries.

Pour the batter into the prepared tin and bake for 35–40 minutes or until golden and firm on top. Remove from the oven and cool in the tin for 15 minutes, then transfer to a wire rack to cool completely. Dust with a little icing sugar and serve with fresh cherries and whipped cream, if you like.

Torta della NONNA

Torta della nonna (Grandma's tart) was not invented by my nonna, or indeed by any specific nonna. Its origins are a little hard to pin down, but it appears the name is meant to convey the tart's intrinsic simplicity and lack of adornment, the way an Italian nonna would make it – a simple pastry case filled with lemony custard and studded with creamy pine nuts. It is absolutely divine and always on offer in dessert carts around Italy.

1 egg white, beaten
100 g (⅔ cup) pine nuts
icing sugar, for dusting
    (optional)

PASTRY
300 g (2 cups) type '00' flour,
    plus extra for dusting
170 g butter, chilled and cut
    into cubes
1 vanilla bean, split and seeds
    scraped
100 g icing sugar
1 egg
1 egg yolk

CUSTARD
750 ml (3 cups) milk
zest of 2 lemons, cut into strips
1 vanilla bean, split and seeds
    scraped
6 egg yolks
170 g (¾ cup) caster sugar
70 g plain flour

SERVES 8–10

To make the pastry, place the flour, butter and vanilla seeds in the bowl of a food processor and pulse until it resembles crumbs. Tip onto a floured board, add the icing sugar and mix well. Make a well in the centre and add the egg and extra yolk. Start incorporating the flour mixture with a fork, then use your hands to bring the dough together. Flatten the dough into a disc and wrap in plastic wrap. Leave to rest in the fridge for 30 minutes.

Meanwhile, to make the custard, pour the milk into a saucepan over medium heat and bring to just below simmering point. Remove from the heat, then add the lemon zest and vanilla bean and seeds. Set aside to cool and infuse for 15 minutes.

In the meantime, beat the egg yolks and caster sugar until pale and fluffy. Add the flour and mix well to remove any lumps. Gently pour the milk mixture through a sieve (to collect the zest and vanilla bean) into the flour mixture and combine well. Pour the mixture back into the pan and cook over low heat for 2–3 minutes until thickened, stirring constantly with a whisk or wooden spoon to remove any lumps. Take it off the heat sooner if you think it's starting to split. Once off the heat, give it a good whisk, then pour into a shallow dish. Cover closely with plastic wrap to prevent a skin forming and leave to cool and thicken.

Preheat your oven to 170°C. Grease and flour a 20 cm springform tin.

Divide the dough into two portions, one slightly larger than the other. Roll out the larger portion to a 3–4 mm thickness and use it to line the base of the prepared tin, making sure the dough reaches 3 cm up the side to create a pastry shell. Pour in the custard, then roll out the second piece of dough to a 3–4 mm thickness and use it to cover the custard. Trim the edge and press to seal, to make sure the custard is well enclosed in the pastry.

Brush the top with the egg white and sprinkle over the pine nuts. Bake for 40–45 minutes until golden. Cool completely in the tin. Remove the side and base of the tin and dust with icing sugar, if you like. Store any leftovers in an airtight container in the fridge for up to 3 days.

Raspberry TART

You say tart, we say crostata, but what really matters is that we all love a good flaky pastry latticed over a sweet, jammy filling. Mamma's recipe for this delicate pastry shell works every time; the trick is to freeze the butter and then whiz everything together in a food processor. It's genius!

250 g (2 cups) raspberries
    (fresh or frozen)
100 g caster sugar (add more
    if you like it very sweet)
20 g butter
1 tablespoon cornflour
1 egg, lightly beaten
granulated sugar, for sprinkling
whipped cream, to serve
    (optional)

FLAKY PASTRY

100 g butter, cut into cubes and
    frozen for 30 minutes
185 g (1¼ cups) plain flour, plus
    extra for dusting
1 tablespoon caster sugar
1–2 tablespoons cold water

SERVES 8–10

Place the raspberries, caster sugar and butter in a saucepan and stir over low heat until the berries have released their natural juices and the liquid has reduced by one-third. This will take about 2–3 minutes. Stir in the cornflour, then cook for a further 2 minutes until the filling starts to thicken. Remove from the heat and allow to cool at room temperature (you can refrigerate it for up to 3 days).

To make the pastry, place the frozen butter cubes, flour and sugar in a food processor and pulse until wet crumbs form. Gradually add the water, starting with 2 teaspoons; keep pulsing and adding more drops of water until you have a soft dough. Tip the dough onto a floured surface and press with your hands to smooth it, then flatten it with your palms to form a disc. Wrap it in plastic wrap and rest in the fridge for a minimum of 30 minutes or up to 3 days.

Preheat your oven to 180°C. Grease and flour a 20 cm tart tin.

Roll out the dough to a 3–4 mm thickness. Cut out a circle slightly larger than the base of the prepared tin, then use it to line the tin, gently pushing it into the edge and up the side to form a rim. Pour in the filling.

Gather up the remaining pastry and roll it out to a 3–4 mm thickness. Cut it into 2 cm wide strips and gently arrange in a lattice pattern over the berry filling. Brush with the beaten egg and sprinkle with some granulated sugar, then bake for 30–35 minutes until golden and gorgeous.

Cool at room temperature and serve as it is or with whipped cream, if desired.

Home-made 'BACI'

Dessert making doesn't have to be complicated. This is more than just a sentiment in Italian home cooking, it's a way of life! We look into our pantries and often the simplest staples are just enough to concoct an impressive dessert, like this homemade version of the famous Baci truffles. If you don't mind getting your hands a little sticky, these mini chocolate bombs can be yours with very little effort. No oven required!

My only advice would be to wait for a cool wintery day to make this treat. Chocolate and hot, sticky summer days don't mix all that well.

80 g roasted hazelnuts, skins removed, plus an extra 16 nuts for topping
1 tablespoon light-tasting olive oil
200 g dark chocolate, chopped
100 g chocolate and hazelnut spread
1 tablespoon Dutch cocoa powder
1 tablespoon Frangelico (optional)

MAKES 16

Use a knife to finely chop the 80 g of hazelnuts. It's better to chop them with a knife, as a blender will likely turn them into a paste. You can also buy pre-chopped hazelnuts if you prefer.

Place the olive oil and 75 g of the chocolate in a heatproof bowl set over a saucepan of simmering water to melt (make sure the bottom of the bowl does not touch the water). Once melted, remove from the heat and add the chocolate and hazelnut spread, cocoa, finely chopped hazelnuts and Frangelico (if using). Mix well, then place in the freezer for about 30–45 minutes to firm up.

Line a tray with baking paper and place a wire rack on top. Take the mixture out of the fridge and shape into 16 walnut-sized bites, then place an extra whole hazelnut on top of each one. Return to the freezer to set for 20 minutes.

Meanwhile, melt the remaining chocolate in a heatproof bowl set over a saucepan of simmering water. Allow it to cool to room temperature.

Take the 'Baci' out of the freezer and place them on the wire rack. Using two forks to help you, dip each one in the melted chocolate to coat completely, then carefully put them back on the rack. Alternatively, place the cooled 'Baci' on the wire rack and pour the chocolate over them. This is particularly effective if friends are watching!

Put the 'Baci' back in the fridge to set for at least 30 minutes, then serve them as they are or wrap in baking paper or foil (don't forget to include a love note in each one!). Store in the fridge for 2–3 days.

Mascarpone, CHOCOLATE AND coffee fingers

If dessert baking falls into the 'too hard' basket for you, let me introduce you to my family's favourite dessert hack, involving no actual baking and measurements that vary according to how many hazelnuts or how much coffee you favour. If you like that famous hazelnut and chocolate spread, then this fudgy slice is for you!

85 g (½ cup) dark chocolate chips
60 g butter, softened
2 tablespoons freshly brewed espresso coffee
1 tablespoon cocoa powder, plus extra for dusting
2 tablespoons brown sugar (or rapadura sugar)
1 vanilla bean, split and seeds scraped
250 g mascarpone
2–3 tablespoons hazelnuts

SERVES 8–10

Melt the chocolate chips and butter in a heatproof bowl set over a saucepan of simmering water (don't let the bottom of the bowl touch the water). Add the coffee, cocoa, sugar and vanilla seeds and mix well to combine. Allow to cool to room temperature, then add the mascarpone and gently beat until incorporated – be careful not to whip it too much or it may split.

Toast the hazelnuts in a frying pan over low heat for 1–2 minutes or until they smell fragrant. Rub them in a tea towel to loosen their skins and set aside to cool for a couple of minutes, then incorporate them into the chocolate mixture.

Line a 20 cm x 10 cm cake tin or baking tray with plastic wrap, leaving a generous overhang on the two long sides. Pour in the batter and flatten with the back of a spoon. Fold the overhanging plastic over the top to enclose it securely, then place in the fridge to set for 2–3 hours.

Turn the slice out onto a board and cut it into roughly 4 cm x 2 cm fingers. Place them in the freezer for 30–45 minutes to set. Serve straight from the freezer, dusted in cocoa powder, with an espresso shot or a little Vin Santo.

Sicilian BRIOCHE

If you've ever travelled around Sicily, you will have undoubtedly encountered this culinary wonder, which, believe it or not, is considered a breakfast dish by locals. It is known in Sicily as 'brioscia col'tuppo' (brioche with a lid), and there is nothing quite like the joy of ripping the lid off and dunking it straight into a pot of traditional granita, or cutting it in half and stuffing it liberally with creamy gelato. Sicilians tend to favour coffee, almond, lemon or the elusive 'gelsi bianchi' (white mulberry) flavours, but I can also personally vouch for raspberry and pistachio. And if you are a bit concerned about having granita or gelato for breakfast, go by my dad's motto: 'se lo mangi a colazione, hai più tempo per smaltirlo' (if you have ice cream in the morning, then you have more time to burn it off). Italian wisdom at its best!

7 g sachet dried yeast
175 ml lukewarm water
550–620 g plain flour,
    plus extra for dusting
3 tablespoons caster sugar
finely grated zest of 1 orange
    and 1 lemon
4 eggs
salt flakes
60 g unsalted butter, cut into
    cubes, softened
1 tablespoon milk
Italian granita or gelato, to serve

MAKES 10

Combine the yeast and lukewarm water in a jug and set aside for 10 minutes or until frothy.

Place the yeast mixture, 550 g of the flour, sugar, orange and lemon zest and 3 eggs in a stand mixer fitted with a dough hook and knead on low speed for 3 minutes to combine. You may need to add a little extra flour, depending on the size of your eggs. Add a pinch of salt and knead for a further 6–7 minutes until smooth.

With the motor running, add the butter, one piece at a time, making sure each piece is incorporated before adding the next, until the dough is smooth and elastic. Transfer to a floured bowl, cover with plastic wrap and set aside for 1½ hours or until doubled in size.

Preheat your oven to 180°C and line two baking trays with baking paper.

Knock back the dough and knead lightly for 30 seconds, then divide it into ten mandarin-sized pieces and six walnut-sized ones. Roll each piece into a smooth ball. Place the large balls on the prepared trays and put the smaller balls on top. Cover the trays with clean tea towels and set aside for a further 20 minutes or until slightly risen.

Whisk the milk and remaining egg in a small bowl. Brush over the brioche, then bake for 20–25 minutes until golden and cooked through. Transfer to a wire rack to cool completely. Serve with your choice of Italian granita or gelato.

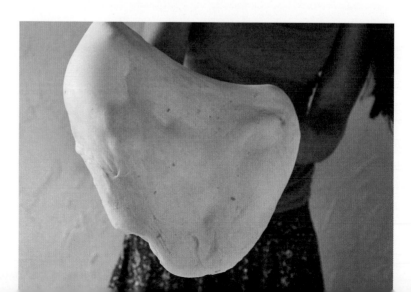

Conversion charts

Measuring cups and spoons may vary slightly from one country to another, but the difference is generally not enough to affect a recipe. All cup and spoon measures are level.

One Australian metric measuring cup holds 250 ml (8 fl oz), one Australian metric tablespoon holds 20 ml (4 teaspoons) and one Australian metric teaspoon holds 5 ml. North America, New Zealand and the UK use a 15 ml (3-teaspoon) tablespoon.

LENGTH

METRIC	IMPERIAL
3 mm	⅛ inch
6 mm	¼ inch
1 cm	½ inch
2.5 cm	1 inch
5 cm	2 inches
18 cm	7 inches
20 cm	8 inches
23 cm	9 inches
25 cm	10 inches
30 cm	12 inches

LIQUID MEASURES

ONE AMERICAN PINT	ONE IMPERIAL PINT
500 ml (16 fl oz)	600 ml (20 fl oz)

CUP	METRIC	IMPERIAL
⅛ cup	30 ml	1 fl oz
¼ cup	60 ml	2 fl oz
⅓ cup	80 ml	2½ fl oz
½ cup	125 ml	4 fl oz
⅔ cup	160 ml	5 fl oz
¾ cup	180 ml	6 fl oz
1 cup	250 ml	8 fl oz
2 cups	500 ml	16 fl oz
2¼ cup	560 ml	20 fl oz
4 cups	1 litre	32 fl oz

DRY MEASURES

The most accurate way to measure dry ingredients is to weigh them. However, if using a cup, add the ingredient loosely to the cup and level with a knife; don't compact the ingredient unless the recipe requests 'firmly packed'.

METRIC	IMPERIAL
15 g	½ oz
30 g	1 oz
60 g	2 oz
125 g	4 oz (¼ lb)
185 g	6 oz
250 g	8 oz (½ lb)
375 g	12 oz (¾ lb)
450 g	16 oz (1 lb)
1 kg	32 oz (2 lb)

OVEN TEMPERATURES

CELSIUS	FAHRENHEIT	CELSIUS	GAS MARK
100°C	200°F	110°C	¼
120°C	250°F	130°C	½
150°C	300°F	140°C	1
160°C	325°F	150°C	2
180°C	350°F	170°C	3
200°C	400°F	180°C	4
220°C	425°F	190°C	5
		200°C	6
		220°C	7
		230°C	8
		240°C	9
		250°C	10

Thank you

Can someone please pinch me? Is this really book number five? What can I say in this section of the book dedicated to gratitude that I haven't said before?

At the risk of repeating myself, I'll give it a go:

Firstly, to my wonderful Pan Macmillan team, brilliantly captained by the formidable Mary Small, whose guidance and hugs I cherish dearly. Jane Winning and Naomi van Groll, thanks for your constant support, sense of humour and for playing with my toddler Luna and puppy Mabel during our hectic shoot.

Rachel Carter, you have been there since book one, with your impeccable eye for typos and inconsistencies! I truly don't know what I would do without you.

Thank you to my brilliant book designer, Emily O'Neill, whose artistry is truly remarkable.

Very special thanks to:

Rob Palmer and Vanessa Austin, my photography/styling duo extraordinaire: how much do I enjoy your company, banter, hilarity and occasional bickering?! You are both amazingly talented and bring such magic to my words and food. And you eat all the leftovers!

Pete Smith, thank you for your kindness and efficiency in the kitchen. And also for cleaning the coffee machine like a pro (only you and I know what I'm talking about ...).

Jono Fleming, who, over the course of the last six years, graduated from assistant to right hand to food producer to actual boss in my kitchen. We are now officially 'bestest of besties'.

To my family, both in Italy and Australia, thanks for your continuous encouragement and love. It is all I ever need and wish for.

To my Aussie and Italian friends, I love you lots and never take you for granted! But please, please, sometimes do cook for me!

And finally, grazie amore mio, e grazie ai miei ragazzi (umani e non). Voi arricchite la mia vita ogni giorno con grande amore, avventure e caos!

Index

V

W

Z

A PLUM BOOK

First published in 2021 by
Pan Macmillan Australia Pty Limited
Level 25, 1 Market Street,
Sydney, NSW, Australia 2000

Level 3, 112 Wellington Parade,
East Melbourne, Victoria, Australia 3002

Design and typesetting by Emily O'Neill
Editing by Rachel Carter
Index by Helena Holmgren
Photography by Rob Palmer
Prop and food styling by Vanessa Austin
Food preparation by Silvia Colloca, Jono Fleming and Pete Smith
Colour reproduction by Splitting Image Colour Studio
Printed and bound in China by Imago Printing International Limited

A CIP catalogue record for this book is available from the National Library of Australia.

10 9 8 7 6 5